Editorial Director ....Lisa Bearnson
Editor ....Tracy White
Administrative Assistant ....Rachael Stone
Contributing Editor ....Alyssa Allgaier
Art Director..Don Lambson
Designer...Joleen Hughes
Production Designers ....Interwest/Rastar; Exposure Graphics
Publisher ....Mark Seastrand
Marketing Director..............................Valerie Dellastatious
Production Manager..Tom Stuber
Wholesale Accounts 800/815-3538
........................Stores A–G ext. 235, Stores H–R ext. 226, Stores S–Z
....and International ext. 244
Advertising..
...................Jenny Grothe, Debbie Hanni, Barbara Tanner, RaNay Winter
----
Cover photo © Michael Carroll

For information on obtaining permission for reprints and excerpts, please contact *Creating Keepsakes* magazine in Orem, UT, at 801/224-8235. For information on ordering *Creating Keepsakes* magazine, call 888/247-5282.

NOTICE OF LIABILITY

TRADEMARKS

Copyright © 2000 Porch Swing Publishing Inc.
All rights reserved. Printed and bound in the U.S.A.
ISBN 1-929180-05-5

THE BIG IDEA BOOK OF
DISNEY MEMORIES

Over 360 Scrapbook Pages

that Celebrate the Happiest

Place on Earth™

D1310763

Porch Swing Publishing Inc.
P.O. Box 469007
Escondido, CA 92046-9007

Toll-free number: 888/247-5282
International: 760/745-2809

CONTENTS

ON THE COVER
"The Thrill of Disney" Page by Brenda Bennett of Morenci, AZ. **Supplies** Patterned paper: Colors By Design; Computer font: CK Journaling, "The Best of Creative Lettering" CD Vol. 2; Lettering idea: Fiesta, The Art of Creative Lettering, Creating Keepsakes Books; Pens: Micron Pigma, Sakura; Milky Gel Roller, Pentel; Colored pencils: Prismacolor, Sanford; Mickey and mouse ears: Brenda got the idea from a piece of Hot Off The Press patterned paper.

Here's to Magical Memories!

Keep your

Disney

adventure

alive

AS A CHILD, I THOUGHT WALT DISNEY was the originator of entertainment. I watched Cinderella, Tom Sawyer and many other classics at the neighborhood theater and didn't miss an episode of "The Wonderful World of Disney" on TV. When I was a junior in high school, my greatest dream came true when I went to Disneyland park with my school band. Instead of ordinary amusement-park attractions like roller coasters, game arcades and Ferris wheels, Disneyland boasted exotic fantasy rides filled with adventure. While I had a great time at the park with my buddies, the only thing missing in my fun-filled day was my family. I vowed then and there that one day I'd bring my parents to Disneyland so they could share in my excitement.

That magical day finally came, and I arrived at Disneyland with my husband, children, parents, in-laws and plenty of film in tow. The excitement of the day was phenomenal—not only was I experiencing the Disney magic through my kids' eyes, I was also seeing it through the eyes of my seventy-something parents! And there's nothing like watching your kids *and* your parents enjoy themselves while you're having a great time too!

Enjoy your ride through this enchanted book. It's filled with magical layouts we've received over the years, layouts from the contest as well as other terrific finds!

Uncle Remus once said, "Everybody's got a laughing place. The trouble is, most folks won't take the time to look for it." Here's to lots of happy laughing places and even more happy memories! ♥

Lisa Bearnson

Take the time to record your family's magical moments in your scrapbook. **Supplies** *Star punches:* McGill (small); Family Treasures (large); *Die cut:* Ellison; *Letter and number stickers:* Repositionable Sticky Die-Cut Letters, Provo Craft; *Pen:* Zig Writer, EK Success.

Paper edge: Corkscrew by Fiskars

Remember the Magic!

WHAT A
CHARACTER

"Getting Goofy at Disneyland"

by Brenée Williams
Boise, ID
Photos by Peggy Peterson
Park City, UT

SUPPLIES

Patterned paper: Debbie Mumm, Creative Imaginations
Lettering template: Kids, Provo Craft
Goofy paper piecing: Brenée's own design
Pen: Zig Fine & Chisel, EK Success
Hole punches: CARL Mfg.

PHOTO OP:

Don't forget to snap
some candid shots of
your kids sizing up
Disney characters.

"Mousin' Around"

by Lori Bergmann
Turlock, CA
Photos by Cindy Yip
San Diego, CA

SUPPLIES

Patterned paper: Paperbilities, MPR
Scissors: Source unknown, Bycin
Lettering template: D.O.T.S.
Circle punch: Family Treasures
Pens: Zig Writers, EK Success; Milky Gel Roller, Pentel
Chalk: Stampin' Up!
Other: Lori cut out a Mickey Mouse postcard and used it on the layout.
Idea to note: Lori used the "Playtime with Mickey and Friends" pattern from Hot Off The Press for Minnie Mouse. She enlarged it to match the size of the Mickey Mouse postcard, then reversed the image and created her own paper-piecing pattern.

"Mickey Mouse"

by Cherilyn A. Johnson
Helper, UT

SUPPLIES

Lettering template: Scrapbook, Provo Craft
Mickey stationery: Paper Pizazz, Hot Off The Press
Number stickers: Sticklers
Pen: The Ultimate Gel Pen, American Crafts
Memorabilia idea: Cherilyn included one of her children's drawings of Mickey Mouse on the layout.

"Here Comes Mickey"

by Sally Garrod

East Lansing, MI

Photos by Emilee Riley

Salt Lake City, UT

S U P P L I E S

Patterned paper: The Paper Patch

Lettering template: Classic, Pebble Tracers, Pebbles in my Pocket

Mickey's gloves template: Sandylion

Mickey paper piecing: Sally got the idea from *Walt Disney's Mickey Mouse Book*, published by Western Pub. Inc.

"Feel the Magic"

by Brenda Bennett

Morenci, AZ

Photos by Peggy Peterson

Park City, UT

S U P P L I E S

Patterned paper: The Paper Patch

Lettering idea: "Flair" from *The Art of Creative Lettering* by Creating Keepsakes Books

Rub-on stars: Provo Craft

Pens: Micron Pigma, Sakura; Zig Writer, EK Success

Computer font: CK Toggle, "The Best of Creative Lettering" CD Vol. 2, *Creating Keepsakes*

Mickey Mouse paper piecing: Brenda adapted it from a children's storybook.

"Hugs from Mickey Mouse"

by Laura Hudson
Boise, ID

SUPPLIES

Photo frame: Frame-Ups, My Mind's Eye
Kids: Friends, My Mind's Eye
Heart punch (mouse-ears hat): Family Treasures
Computer fonts: CK Fill In and CK Calligraphy, "The Best of
Creative Lettering" CD Vol. 1, *Creating Keepsakes*

"Mickey"

by Jenny Jackson
Arlington, VA
Photo by Peggy Peterson
Park City, UT
SUPPLIES

Patterned paper: The Paper Patch
Lettering template: Block Serif,
Pebble Tracers, Pebbles in my Pocket
Disney characters stationery:
Paper Pizazz, Hot Off The Press
Pen: Zig Writer, EK Success

Mickey signing Matthew's hat!

"Mickey Signing Matthew's Hat"

by Jennifer Nye
Hamilton, OH
SUPPLIES

Alphabet stickers: Creative Memories
Corner punch: Crown, McGill
Pen: Micron Pigma, Sakura
Idea to note: Jennifer took a picture of
Matthew's hat and included it on the layout.

"Mickey—Love at First Sight"
by Brenda Cosgrove
Pebbles in my Pocket
Orem, UT
SUPPLIES

Patterned paper: The Paper Patch
Lettering template: Block, ABC Tracers, EK Success
Bow and circles die cuts: Pebbles in my Pocket
Hole punch: Punchline, McGill
Computer font: Scrap Swirl, Lettering Delights Vol. 1,
Inspire Graphics
Hearts: Brenda's own designs

"Magical Moment"
by Sandy Thigpin
Vancouver, WA
SUPPLIES

Photo frame: Frame-Ups, My Mind's Eye
Computer fonts: CK Anything Goes, "The Best of
Creative Lettering" CD Vol. 1, *Creating Keepsakes* (title);
Comic Sans, Microsoft Word (journaling)
Die cuts: Pebbles in my Pocket
Pen: Zig Scroll & Brush, EK Success

Paper edge: Corkscrew by Fiskars

"We Love Mickey"

by Kari Murphy
Scrappin' Peeps
Olympia, WA

SUPPLIES

Patterned paper: PrintWorks

Embossed paper: Lasting Impressions for Paper

Border stickers: me & my BIG ideas

Title lettering: Kari got the idea from Scrappers' AlphaBook

Alphabet letters: "Kids" Alphabitties, Repositionable Sticky Die-Cut Letters, Provo Craft

Pen: Zig Writer, EK Success

Memorabilia idea: Kari included postcards from her Disney trip on the layout.

"Welcome To My World"

by Judith Anderson
Blue Springs, MO

SUPPLIES

Mickey Mouse fold-out: Hallmark Crown Disney Card, Hallmark

Photo frames: Frame-Ups, My Mind's Eye

Alphabet letters: Geographics

Die cuts: Accu-Cut Systems

Scissors: Seagull edge, Fiskars

Pen: Zig Writer, EK Success

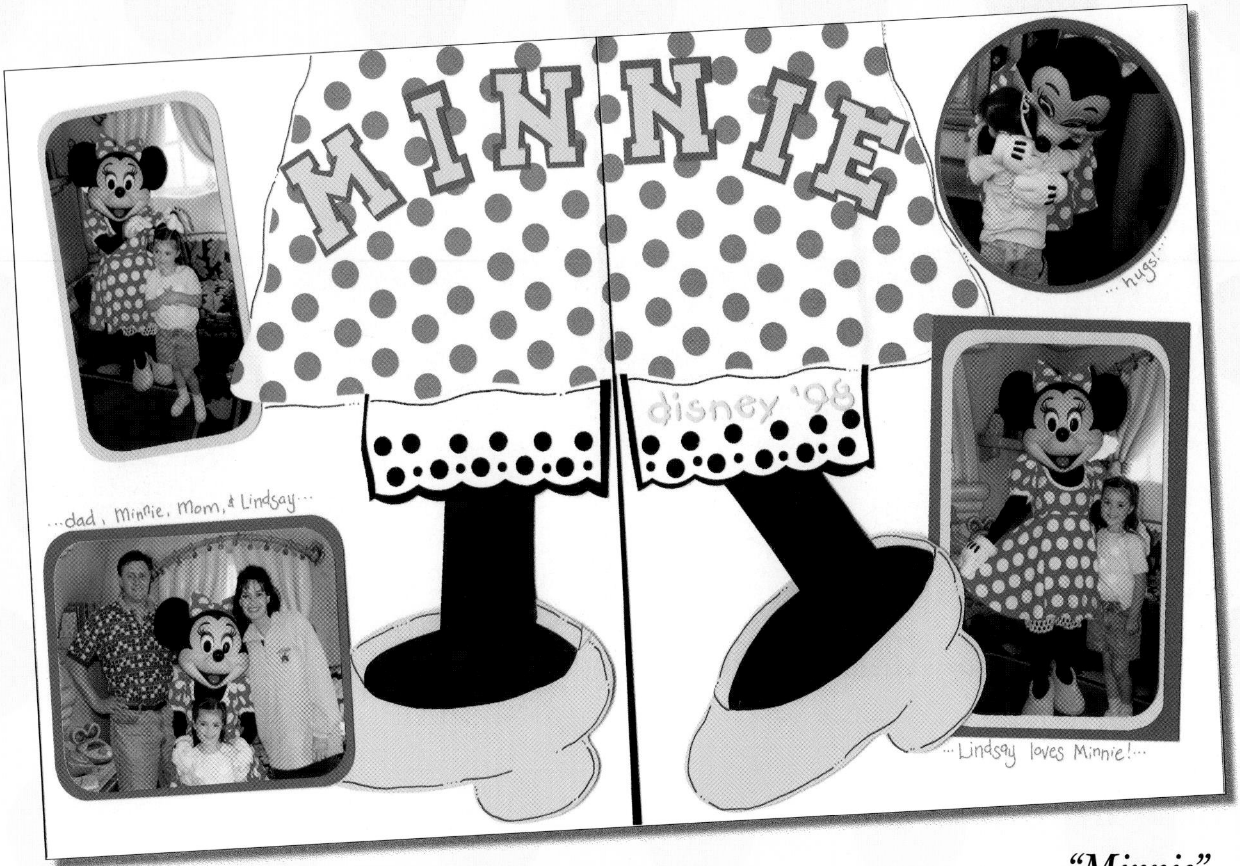

MINNIE
disney '98
...hugs!...
...dad, Minnie, Mom, & Lindsay...
...Lindsay loves Minnie!...

"Minnie"

by Alycia Alvarez
Altus, OK
Photos by Laurie Green
Alpine, UT

SUPPLIES

Patterned paper: The Paper Patch
Lettering template: Block Serif, Pebble Tracers, Pebbles in my Pocket
Alphabet letters: "Kids" Alphabitties, Repositionable Sticky Die-Cut Letters, Provo Craft
Hole punches: Punchline, McGill
Pens: Hybrid Gel Roller, Pentel; Zig Millennium, EK Success

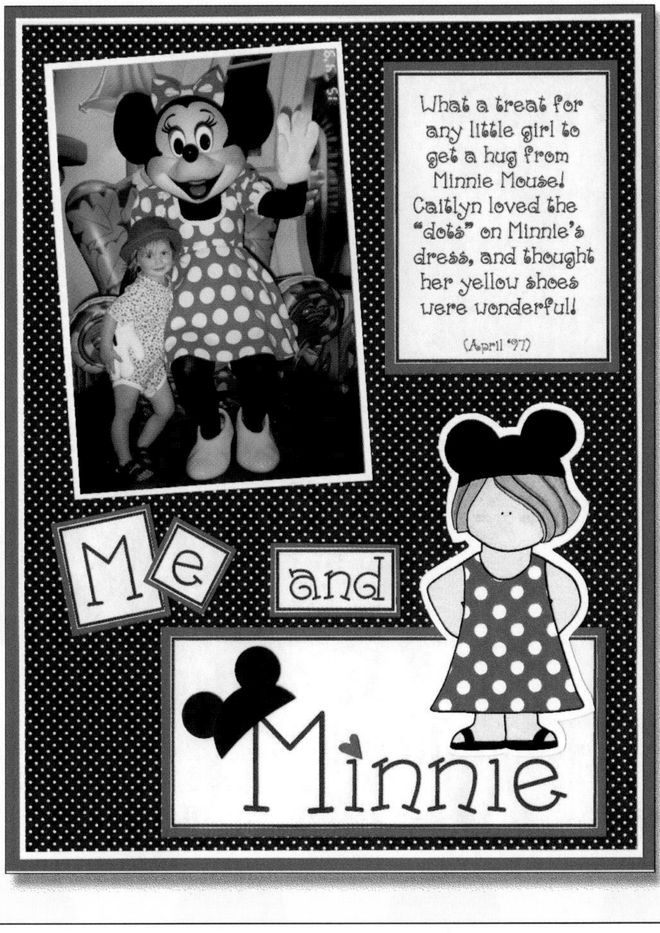

What a treat for any little girl to get a hug from Minnie Mouse! Caitlyn loved the "dots" on Minnie's dress, and thought her yellow shoes were wonderful!
(April '97)
Me
and
Minnie

"Me and Minnie"

by Brenda Cosgrove
Pebbles in my Pocket
Orem, UT

SUPPLIES

Patterned paper: The Paper Patch
Girl accent: Friends, My Mind's Eye
Computer font: Scrap Swirl, Lettering Delights Vol. 1, Inspire Graphics
Circle punch: Family Treasures

Paper edge: Corkscrew by Fiskars

"Camp Minnie and Mickey"

by Demetria Edwards
St. Augustine, FL
SUPPLIES

Wood patterned paper: Provo Craft
Letter die cuts: Scrapbook, Accu-Cut Systems
Pen: Zig Writer, EK Success
Mickey and Minnie paper piecing: Demetria got the idea
from a Disney coloring book.

"We Love Mickey"

by Beth Wakulsky
Haslett, MI
Photos by Jeanne English
Salt Lake City, UT
SUPPLIES

Patterned paper: The Paper Patch
Lettering template: Fat Caps, Frances Meyer
Mickey hands: Adapted from the "Baby, Baby" template by Provo Craft
Heart: "Heart" Micro Template, Provo Craft
Computer font: DJ Crazed, Fontastic! Vol. 2, D.J. Inkers

What a find!
Mickey and Minnie
on our 1st day in
the park. Ryan
and Scott were
so excited.

"Mickey and Minnie"

by Ann Burton
Magna, UT
SUPPLIES
Lettering template: Zoom, Close To My Heart/D.O.T.S.
Mickey accent stationery: Paper Pizazz, Hot Off The Press
Pen: Zig Writer, EK Success

"Goofy Ducks"

by Sally Garrod
East Lansing, MI
Photos by Jeanne English
Salt Lake City, UT
SUPPLIES
Alphabet letters: Fat Dot, Repositionable Sticky Die-Cut Letters, Provo Craft

Star and Design Line stickers: Mrs. Grossman's
Punches (large star, egg and circles): Family Treasures
Hole punches (oval and circle): Punchline, McGill
Computer font: DJ Doodlers, Fantastic! Vol. 1, D.J. Inkers

Scrooge teaches the English children "High Finance." His number on tip, "Save your pennies!" Laurie, Nik, Scrooge, Amy, Audrey and Emilee (above, left to right).
Audrey, Scrooge and Nik (left).

Daisy Duck can make the family smile. Emilee, Audrey, Laurie, Amy, Daisy and Nik (above, left to right).
Daisy and Laurie, a couple of cute chicks (left).

Disneyland
October, 1989

Paper edge: Corkscrew by Fiskars

"Quack Attack"

by Shannon Wolz
Salt Lake City, UT
Photo by Peggy Peterson
Park City, UT

S U P P L I E S

Patterned paper: Provo Craft
Vivelle sponge paper
(Donald Duck's body): Wintech
Lettering template: Block Serif, Pebble
Tracers, Pebbles in my Pocket
Egg punch (eyes): Marvy Uchida
Computer font: CK Toggle,
"The Best of Creative Lettering"
CD Vol. 2, *Creating Keepsakes*
Donald Duck paper piecing:
Shannon's own design

When Tana was three, we took her to DISNEYLAND for her first time. This is one of my very favorite photos of her. Whenever Tana looks at this photo she says, "Donald is telling me a secret!"

"Ducky Love"

by Julie Coons Anderson
Renton, WA

S U P P L I E S

Letter die cuts: Vagabond, Ellison
Button die cuts: Ellison
Pen: Zig Writer, EK Success
Computer fonts:
downloaded off the Internet
Bow, collar and small buttons:
Julie's own designs

Paper-piecing art by Brenée Williams of Boise, ID

Vacation Tip

♥

Looking for a romantic getaway?
Walt Disney World is one of
the most popular honeymoon
destinations in the country—you
can even tie the knot there!
For more information,
call 407/828-3400.

ELIZABETH BURDETT & DONALD
January 1999
Disneyland

Goofy

Disneyland January 2000

SHERIFF

"Sheriff Goofy"
by Christine Walker
Provo, UT
S U P P L I E S
Sheriff's badge and hat accents: PagePieces,
Cock-A-Doodle Design Inc.
Patterned paper: The Paper Patch
Scissors (on lasso): Mammoth Scallop edge,
Paper Adventures
Pens: Zig Writers, EK Success
Lasso: Christine's own design
Other: Christine enlarged her photo
using the Kodak Picture Maker.

"Morgan Loves Goofy"
by Melodie Jones
Yorba Linda, CA
S U P P L I E S
Lettering template: Jungle-Letters,
Better Letter Templates, The Crafter's Workshop
Pen: Zig Writer, EK Success
Computer font: CK Journaling, "The Best of
Creative Lettering" CD Vol. 2, *Creating Keepsakes*
Goofy paper piecing: Melodie used a graphic from the Disney web site.

MORGAN + GOOFY

September 12, 1999
Goofy is Morgan's favorite Disney character. While she stood in line to get his autograph, I told Goofy's helper that he was her favorite. The helper then told Goofy, who immediately started hugging Morgan and licking her head. She loved it! This is what he wrote in her book:

TO my bestest pal in the whole world ♥ Goofy

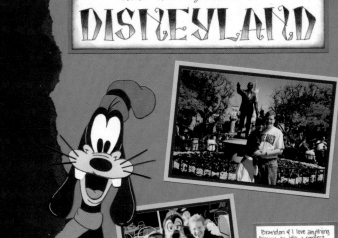

our "Hunnymoon" to
DISNEYLAND

Brandon & I love anything Disney, so it's a perfect "Hunnymoon" for us! We spent five days in Disneyland and never got sick of it! We went on every ride—some multiple times of course! We went shopping and if we saw something we wanted (but couldn't afford) we'd take a picture of it! Disneyland is the happiest place on earth and the perfect place to be in love!

March 27–April 3
1 9 9 6

"Our 'Hunnymoon' to Disneyland"
by Brenda Bennett
Morenci, AZ
Photos by Emilee Riley
Salt Lake City, UT
S U P P L I E S
Lettering idea: "Fiesta" from *The Art of Creative*
Lettering by Creating Keepsakes Books
Goofy paper piecing: Brenda's own design
Colored pencils: Prismacolor, Sanford
Pens: Hybrid Gel Roller, Pentel; Micron Pigma, Sakura
Ink pad (sponging of title): Personal Stamp Exchange

"Goofy"

by Grace T. Breeden
A Page In Time
Lincoln, NE
S U P P L I E S
Patterned paper:
Paper Adventures
Goofy stationery: Paper
Pizazz, Hot Off The Press

Lettering template: Hand
Drawn, Pebble Tracers,
Pebbles in my Pocket
Scissors: Heartstrings edge,
Fiskars
Pen: Zig Millennium,
EK Success

"We Love Pluto"

by Therese Woozley
Boise, ID
S U P P L I E S
Computer fonts: Scrap Outline
and Scrap Sister, Lettering
Delights Vol. 3, Inspire Graphics
Scissors: Jigsaw edge, Fiskars
*Mickey balloon die cut (cut in

half for mouse-ears hat):*
Accu-Cut Systems
*Donald Duck hat and tea cup
accents:* Cut from a PageTopper
from Cock-A-Doodle Design Inc.
Pluto paper piecing: Therese's
own design

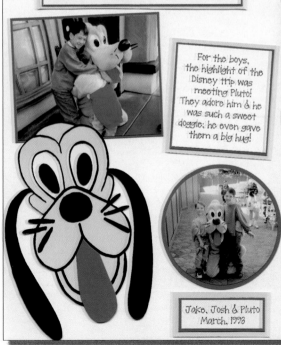

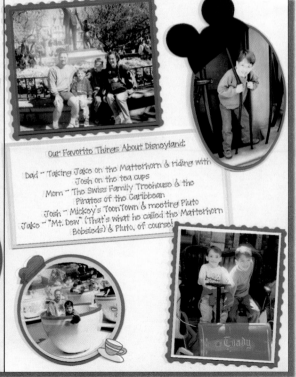

Pluto tickled kids of all ages.

We were all too excited to eat our delicious Disney breakfast.

Terry & Wanda, Larry & Cathy, Myrtle & Harry, Mom & Dad, and Fred & I had every bit as much fun as Gigi, Jeremy, & Alicia did.

Pluto was our favorite. He was wild with joy. He played and cavorted with everyone.

Pluto knew that the finest thing of all was just to be Mickey's Dog.

Breakfast with the Characters

"Pluto"
by Joyce Hill Schweitzer
Greensboro, NC
SUPPLIES
Patterned paper: Keeping Memories Alive (beige striped and speckled); Northern Spy (plaid and striped with stars)
Alphabet letters: Creative Memories
Rubber stamps: Northern Spy (starburst patch); Delta Technical Coatings (Mickey Mouse)
Ink pad: ColorBox, Clearsnap Inc.
Yellow embossing powder (on block stamps): Mark Enterprises
Scissors: Deckle edge, Family Treasures
Pens: Tombow; Micron Pigma, Sakura; Zig Opaque Writer, EK Success
Pluto paper piecing: Joyce's own design (based on Disney storybooks)
Bone, bowl and Mickey balloons: Joyce's own designs

or "Fluto" as Lauren called him.

Breakfast with... PLUTO! Eric was so excited to meet him. Lauren liked him too - from a distance. Pluto tried to win her over, but she was a hard sell! Nov. 98

"Meeting Pluto"
by Marla Bird
Pebbles in my Pocket
Orem, UT
SUPPLIES
Lettering template: Block, ABC Tracers, EK Success
Pluto paper piecing: Marla's own design
Pen: Zig Writer, EK Success

"Jaena Loves Pooh, Tigger and Eeyore"

by Lanae Beth Johnson
Glendale, AZ

SUPPLIES

Pen: Zig Writer, EK Success

Idea to note: Lanae enlarged some of her photos to create better focal points.

"Pooh, Tigger and Eeyore Autographs"

by Ellen James
Orem, UT

SUPPLIES

Winnie the Pooh stickers: Sandylion

Memorabilia idea: Ellen included autographs from the Disney characters next to their photos.

Deep in the Hundred Acre Wood

In November 1996, we went to Disneyland for Thanksgiving. We had a great time meeting of the characters & riding all of the kiddie rides!

"Deep in the Hundred-Acre Wood"

by Jenny Jackson
Arlington, VA
S U P P L I E S
Patterned paper: Provo Craft
Computer font: CK Chunky (title) and
CK Journaling (journaling), "The Best
of Creative Lettering" CD Vol. 2,
Creating Keepsakes

Cloud die cuts: Ellison
Bee and beehive rub-ons: Provo Craft
Scissors: Grass edge, Provo Craft
Tree: Jenny's own design

"Winnie the Pooh and Tigger Too"

by Karen Petersen
Mom and Me Scrapbooking
Salt Lake City, UT
Photos by Laurie Green
Alpine, UT
S U P P L I E S
Patterned paper:
The Paper Patch
Circle punches (bees):
Family Treasures

Computer font: Scrap Simple,
Lettering Delights Vol. 2,
Inspire Graphics
Pen: Zig Writer, EK Success
Bees: Karen's own design
Other: Karen cut Winnie the
Pooh and Tigger out of Disney
postcards and included them
on the layout.

Winnie the Pooh and Tigger Too

Towards the end of the day, we finally found Tigger and Pooh! Lindsay ran up to Pooh and hugged him for the longest time. Then she gave Tigger an equally long hug. On our way back to the hotel that night she told me... "Mommy, I love Pooh." Don't we all?

PAPER ADVENTURES ®

Pretty
Pri

Paper piecing…colorful and fun with Diamond Dust™ and other Coordinates™ scrapbooking products from Paper Adventures.

Belle, Snow White, Aurora, Cinderella, Mulan or Jasmine – which is your little girl's favorite Disney heroine?

Whether your princess takes part in a royal pageant or just likes to play dress-up, a four-page storybook layout can feature her pretty photos.

These pages feature many Paper Adventures exclusive products that are fit for any princess, including Diamond Dust™, Velveteen Paper™ and Two-Tone Archivals™.

Look for a complete materials list for "Diamond Dust Fairy Tale" on our web site.

Princess paper piecing ideas from *Disney's Princess Collection, Love and Friendship Stories* by Disney Press NY, NY.

DIAMOND DUST FAIRY TALE™

Clip & Save IDEA STARTER™

PAPER ADVENTURES PRODUCT GUIDE

Diamond Dust™ Diamond Dust in Daffodil, Sunflower, Blueberry and Wedgwood gave us spectacular sparkle for the princesses' gowns. Look for new Metallic Diamond Dust colors Gold Nugget and Sterling, and coordinating Diamond Dust Prints!

Two-Tone Archivals™ We used versatile, two-sided Two-Tones in Peaches 'n' Cream for skin tones.

Velveteen Paper™ Velveteen Paper in Licorice, Mocha and Wheat have color and texture that are perfect for beautiful hair. Velveteen Paper is easy to cut and can be heat-embossed with a rubber stamp and a hot iron.

Punch Wheel™ We punched a variety of stars using the easy-to-use Punch Wheel – six punches in one handy tool! New Two Wheelers™ give you twice as many shape options – in Zoo and Harvest themes.

Punch Wheel "Two Wheelers"

Big 'Boss™ Our new paper crimping tool gave us texture for the picture frames. Also available: new Lil 'Boss in Diamond, Heart, Ring and Wave patterns.

'Boss embossing tools

Diamond Dust

Parchlucent™ Paper We punched Pearl Parchlucent to create shining, translucent stars.

Mix 'n' Match Archivals™ Sunflower, a new color in the Mix 'n' Match family, was used for bright frames and the banner. Look for additional new classic colors like Ruby, Orchid and Avocado.

Storybook Page Protectors™
Preserve your fairy tale in a four-page Storybook Protector.

PAPER ADVENTURES®
BEGIN YOUR ADVENTURE TODAY!
1-800-727-0699
www.paperadventures.com

Dealers, call for info on becoming a Paper Adventures Authorized Retailer. Consumers in your area will be directed to your store.

The kids were so delighted to add their favorite characters to their autograph books. Tyler's favorite was Tigger!

Hidden away in the Hundred-Acre Wood we discovered Pooh, Tigger & Eeyore!

"It's So Much Friendlier with Pooh"

by Amber Blakesley
Provo, UT
Photos by Valerie Dellastatious
Orem, UT
SUPPLIES

Patterned paper: Northern Spy
Scissors: Pinking edge, Wiss
Lettering template: Block, ABC Tracers, EK Success
Pen: Micron Pigma, Sakura
Flowers and bees: Amber's own designs

"Eeyore and Me"

by Valerie Dellastatious
Orem, UT
SUPPLIES

Eeyore stationery: Paper Pizazz, Hot Off The Press
Computer font: CK Toggle, "The Best of Creative Lettering" CD Vol. 2, *Creating Keepsakes*

Eeyore and me!

I posed with my favorite Winnie the Pooh character, Eeyore. I was the oldest one in line, but Eeyore didn't seem to mind.
Walt Disney World, October 1999

Paper edge: Corkscrew by Fiskars

"It's Much Friendlier with Two"

by Brenda Bennett
Morenci, AZ
Photos by Emilee Riley
Salt Lake City, UT
S U P P L I E S

Computer font: DJ Serif, Dazzle Days, D.J. Inkers
Pens: Zig Writers, EK Success; Micron Pigma, Sakura
Circle punches: Family Treasures
Colored pencils: Prismacolor, Sanford
Vellum: The Paper Company
Bees and "hunny" pot: Brenda's own designs
Title: Brenda's own design

"Pooh, Eeyore, You 'n Tigger Too"

by Sally Garrod
East Lansing, MI
Photos by Peggy Peterson
Park City, UT
S U P P L I E S

Lettering template: Block, ABC Tracers, EK Success
Cloud die cuts: Pebbles in my Pocket
Spiral punch: All Night Media
Computer font: CK Journaling, "The Best of Creative Lettering" CD Vol. 2, *Creating Keepsakes*
Pencil and notepad: Sally's own designs

"Eyore"

by Grace T. Breeden
A Page In Time
Lincoln, NE
S U P P L I E S

Patterned paper: Paper Adventures
Lettering template: Hand Drawn,
Pebble Tracers, Pebbles in my Pocket
Scissors: Pinking edge, Fiskars
Pen: Zig Millennium, EK Success
Eyore paper piecing: Grace's own design

"Peek-a-Boo with Eyore"

by Kathy V. Vernon
Coalville, UT
S U P P L I E S

Patterned paper: Provo Craft
Alphabet letters: "Kids" Alphabitties,
Repositionable Sticky Die-Cut Letters, Provo Craft
Die-cut letters: remember when . . ., Colorbök
Square punch: All Night Media
Eyore stationery: Paper Pizazz, Hot Off The Press
Pen: Hybrid Gel Roller, Pentel

"Bouncin' with Tigger"
by Laurie Carley
Centralia, WA
S U P P L I E S
Tigger accent: A Disney postcard
Computer fonts: Steamer and Scribble, Print Shop Deluxe
Idea to note: Laurie created Tigger's bounce springs with black wire.

"Our 'Hunny'moon"
by Shannon Wolz
Salt Lake City, UT
Photos by Emilee Riley
Salt Lake City, UT
S U P P L I E S
Lettering template: Kids, Provo Craft
Heart and moon template: Provo Craft
Punches: Punchline (flower),
Gemline (small circle), McGill (flower)
Computer font: CK Script, "The Best of Creative
Lettering" CD Vol. 1, *Creating Keepsakes*
Pooh and "hunny" pot: Shannon's own designs

Paper edge: Corkscrew by Fiskars

"Ariel's Grotto™"

by Lori Bergmann
Turlock, CA
Photos by Laurie Green
Alpine, UT

S U P P L I E S

Patterned paper: Provo Craft
Ariel stationery: Paper Pizazz, Hot Off The Press
Vellum: Paper Adventures
Scissors: Jumbo Wave edge, Provo Craft
Lettering idea: "Funky Wave" from *The Art of Creative Lettering* by Creating Keepsakes Books
Pen: Zig Writer, EK Success
Colored pencils: Prismacolor, Sanford
Seaweed: Lori's own design

"Little Mermaid"

by Kathy Mancini
San Jose, CA

S U P P L I E S

Patterned paper: Paper Adventures
Lettering template: Classic, Pebble Tracers, Pebbles in my Pocket
Starfish die cut: Ellison
Seaweed: Kathy's own design
Computer font: CK Print, "The Best of Creative Lettering" CD Vol. 1, *Creating Keepsakes*
Pen: Zig Millennium, EK Success

"Under the Sea"

by Karen Glenn
Orem, UT
Photos by
Valerie Dellastatious
Orem, UT
S U P P L I E S
Lettering template: Rounded,
Pebble Tracers,
Pebbles in my Pocket

Hole punch: Punchline, McGill
Pen: Gelly Roll, Sakura
Notes and starfish: Karen's
own designs
Idea to note: Karen padded
the starfish to give them
depth.

"Ariel and Bryanne"

by Heather Thatcher
Draper, UT
Photos by Cindy Yip
San Diego, CA
S U P P L I E S
Lettering idea: "Flair" from *The Art of Creative*
Lettering by Creating Keepsakes Books
Pen: Zig Writer, EK Success
Colored pencils: Prismacolor, Sanford
Scissors: Microtip, Fiskars
Grass and starfish: Heather's own designs
Ink pad (for brayered background paper):
Kaleidacolor, Tsukineko
Idea to note: Heather got the idea to make
her own patterned paper using the brayered
technique from Posh Impressions.

Paper-piecing art by
Brenée Williams of Boise, ID

Paper edge: Corkscrew by Fiskars

"Dining with Cinderella"

by Ellen James
Orem, UT

SUPPLIES

Die cuts: Accu-Cut Systems (castle); Cut-it-Up (knight)
Stickers: Mrs. Grossman's
Computer font: CK Calligraphy,
"The Best of Creative Lettering" CD Vol. 1,
Creating Keepsakes

"Cinderella Is My Favorite Princess"

by Missy Jaycox
St. Louis, MO

SUPPLIES

Pen: Zig Writer, EK Success
Castle accent: Missy cut the castle accents
from a Disney brochure.

They said you were "Sleeping Beauty" the day you arrived, Alyssa, but just look at you at Disneyland on your 5th Halloween. You look just like Cinderella and you weren't shy to meet her. You got her autograph, listened to her read a story, modeled your dresses and even got a hug! We wonder what you'll be when you grow up...

"Cinderella"

by Debi Adams

Anaheim, CA

S U P P L I E S

Patterned paper: Making Memories

Ink pads: Close To My Heart/D.O.T.S. (pastels); D.O.T.S. (black)

Rubber stamps: Close To My Heart/D.O.T.S. (Pizazz alphabet, Dress-Up, Ballet); Darcy Hunter (castle)

Silver pen: Hybrid Gel Roller, Pentel

Heart stickers: Stickopotamus

Star punch: McGill

Watercolor pencils: Derwent

"Cinderella"

by Rachel Norton

Mesa, AZ

S U P P L I E S

Mulberry paper: PrintWorks

Lettering template: Brush template, C-Thru Stencils, The C-Thru Ruler Co.

Design template (for pearls): Romantic, Memories Forever, Westrim

Computer font: CK Script, "The Best of Creative Lettering" CD Vol. 1, *Creating Keepsakes*

Pen: Gelly Roll, Sakura

Other: Rachel adhered pearls and gold fasteners to the layout for enhancements.

When Jeff, Caroline, and Sarah arrived at the entrance to Cinderella's Castle, Sarah was terrified to go inside. She was afraid that Cinderella's wicked stepsisters would be there! Caroline and Jeff tried to reason her but there was no calming her. The Disney employees working at the castle entrance noticed that she was upset and asked what was wrong. When Caroline and Jeff said that Sarah was afraid that the wicked stepsisters would be inside, the employees said assuringly, "Oh no! We never let them come anywhere near here. We don't ever let them inside." Sarah was still a little unsure but decided to give it a try. Once she saw Cinderella and the Fairy Godmother (and no wicked stepsisters), she relaxed and had a fun time.

"I Want to Be a Disney Princess"

by Jennifer McCloskey
Fishers, IN
SUPPLIES

Diamond Dust paper: Paper Adventures
Punches: Family Treasures
Scissors: MaxiScallop edge, MaxiCuts,
Making Memories; Notch and
Victorian edges, Fiskars
Stamps (clouds and castle squares): D.O.T.S.
Ink pad: D.O.T.S.
Other: Jennifer used silver ribbons for borders
and a pink ribbon for the princess hat.

Ideas to note: Jennifer sponged acid-free blue
paint from Delta Technical Coatings on the
layout to create the sky. She used clear
embossing ink and glitter to create the
sparkles on the castle and background.

"Natalie Meets Alice"

by Linda Foster
Williamsville, NY
SUPPLIES

Patterned paper: Paper Pizazz,
Hot Off The Press
Daisy punch: Marvy Uchida
Computer fonts: CK Anything Goes and CK
Print, "The Best of Creative Lettering" CD
Vol. 1, *Creating Keepsakes*
Colored pencils: Memory
Pencils, EK Success
Pens: Zig Millennium and
Zig Writer, EK Success
Scissors: Scallop edge, Fiskars
Alice paper piecing: Linda's own design
(based on a picture in a Disney book)

"Hi-Ho, Hi-Ho to Disneyland We Go"

by Jennifer Jensen
Hurricane, UT
Photos by Laurie Green
Alpine, UT

SUPPLIES

Lettering template: Block, ABC Tracers, EK Success
Patterned paper: Keeping Memories Alive
Suede paper (on dwarfs): Paper Adventures
Pen: Zig Memory System, EK Success
Colored pencils: Memory Pencils, EK Success
Ink pad (for rosy cheeks and noses): ColorBox, Clearsnap Inc.
Dwarfs paper piecing: Jennifer's own designs (adapted from children's storybook)

"Jaena and Cinderella"

by **Lanae Beth Johnson**
Glendale, AZ
SUPPLIES
Balloon die cut: Accu-Cut Systems
Pen: Micron Pigma, Sakura

"Ladies Man"

by Kristina Williams
Pebbles in my Pocket
Orem, UT
S U P P L I E S
Lettering template: Block,
ABC Tracers, EK Success
Punches: Marvy Uchida (heart);
McGill (circle)
Hole punch: Punchline, McGill
Pen: Zig Writer, EK Success

"Madeline's Princess Collection"

by Jennifer McLaughlin
Back Door Friends—The Scrapbooking Company
Whittier, CA
S U P P L I E S
Patterned paper: Sonburn
Vellum: ANW Crestwood
Princess hats: Jennifer's own designs
Pens: Zig Writer, EK Success;
Hybrid Gel Roller, Pentel
Colored pencils: Prismacolor, Sanford
Lettering idea: "Gala" from *The Art of Creative
Lettering* by Creating Keepsakes Books
Other: Jennifer used gold and white
ribbons on the princess hats.

"A Whole New World"

by Julie Coons Anderson
Renton, WA
SUPPLIES
Cloud background paper: Paper
Pizazz, Hot Off The Press
Specialty paper: DMD Industries
(corrugated paper); Personal
Stamp Exchange (mulberry paper);
The Paper Company (vellum);
Paper Adventures (Diamond Dust)
Alphabet letters: Funky,
Repositionable Sticky Die-Cut
Letters, Provo Craft
Cloud die cuts: Ellison
Computer font: Calligrapher,
downloaded from the Internet
Flying carpets: Julie's own design

"Aladdin"

by Faye Carnahan
Midvale, UT
SUPPLIES
Lettering template: Wacky Letters,
Frances Meyer
Speckled paper: Paper Adventures
Vellum: Paper Adventures
Scissors: Ripple edge, Fiskars
Lantern: Faye's own design

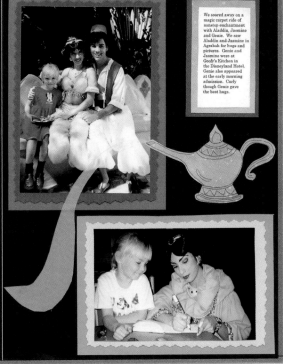

We soared away on a
magic carpet ride of
nonstop enchantment
with Aladdin, Jasmine
and Genie. We saw
Aladdin and Jasmine in
Agrabah for hugs and
pictures. Genie and
Jasmine were at
Goofy's Kitchen in
the Disneyland Hotel.
Genie also appeared
at the early morning
admission. Carly
though Genie gave
the best hugs.

"A Whole New World"

by Alycia Alvarez
Altus, OK
Photos by Laurie Green
Alpine, UT

S U P P L I E S

Patterned paper: Keeping Memories Alive
(yellow plaid); Provo Craft (yellow checked)
Corner slot punch: Double Scallop, Family Treasures
Pen: Le Plume, Marvy Uchida
Colored pencils: Memory Pencils, EK Success
Computer fonts: CK Script and CK Fill In, "The Best of
Creative Lettering" CD, Vol. 1, *Creating Keepsakes*
World: Alycia's own design
Other: Alycia printed the genie from her
computer and colored him with markers.

"Beauty and the Beast Autographs"

by Ellen James
Orem, UT

S U P P L I E S

Stickers: Sandylion (Beauty and the Beast);
Mrs. Grossman's (rose)
Pens: Zig Writers, EK Success
Memorabilia idea: Ellen included
autographs from the Disney characters
next to their photos.

"Our Beauty Meets Belle"

by Cynthia Castelluccio
Carrollton, VA

SUPPLIES

Vellum: Paper Adventures
Corner edger: Regal, Fiskars
Memorabilia pocket: 3L Corp.
Pens: Pen-touch, Sakura
3-D rose die cuts: Cynthia got the idea from *Memory Makers* magazine.
Memorabilia idea: Cynthia included a Belle souvenir penny on the layout.

Vacation Tip

Looking for characters?
Head over to Mickey's
Toontown, where a lot of them
are available for
autographs.

Paper-piecing art by
Brenée Williams of Boise, ID

"Lindsay and Belle"

by Karen Glenn
Orem, UT
Photos by Laurie Green
Alpine, UT

SUPPLIES

Patterned paper: Keeping Memories Alive
Diamond Dust paper (inside flowers):
Paper Adventures
Punches: All Night Media (spiral); McGill (circle); Family Treasures (daisy for leaves)
Pens: Zig Writers, EK Success

Meeting Mulan

Kaylee took her Mulan Halloween costume to DisneyWorld, to wear during the Mulan parade at MGM Studios. During the parade, several performers saw her, waved and said, "Hi, Mulan!" When Mulan and Shang spotted her, they blew kisses. Kaylee beamed the whole day. When we discovered Mulan signing autographs that night, Kaylee climbed back into her costume and got in line. We wondered if Mulan would remember her, and did she ever! She hugged Kaylee and said, "I saw you at the parade today. You look SO beautiful. Are you going to the matchmaker? Here's some advice: don't set her on fire!" After hugs and kisses, Mulan signed her autograph book and pressed a kiss on the page. She told Kaylee to "be brave and strong and grow up to do what you truly want." What a wonderful day. We all felt special.

"Meeting Mulan"
by Karen Madigan
Green River, WY
SUPPLIES

Specialty papers: Kodak (pink glitter);
Pebbles in my Pocket (blue metallic)
Computer font: Flatbrush, Print Artist Gold 4.0
Stickers: Hallmark (Mulan stickers);
Mrs. Grossman's (Design Lines and hearts)

"Mulan"
by Caprice Rosales
Daly City, CA
SUPPLIES

Vellum: Frances Meyer
Pens: Zig Opaque Writers, EK Success
Mulan characters: Caprice cut them out
of a Little Golden Book story of Mulan.
Title: Caprice traced the title from a storybook onto vellum.
Lantern, clouds, flowers and tree: Caprice's own designs

DISNEYLAND 1998
MULAN

Magical Memories

O'Scrap!™

a division of Imaginations!

Disney characters © Disney Enterprises, Inc.

Keep the magic alive with O'Scrap!™ Our line of frames, die-cuts and background papers make it easy to capture your memories of the Happiest Place on Earth™!

801-225-6015 Fax: 801-225-6899 ♥ www.imaginations-inc.com ♥ e-mail: buyme@imaginations-inc.com

When Trent met The Green Army Man STRANGE things happened. First, Trent's hat was removed from his head and placed on Alan's head. Then the Army Man took Trent for a stroll down the streets of MGM Studios.

"Toy Story"

by Karen Wills
Jackson, MO

SUPPLIES

Alphabet letters: "Scrapbook" and "Fat Dot" Alphabitties, Repositionable Sticky Die-Cut Letters, Provo Craft

Toy Story accents: Punch-Outs, Hot Off The Press

Star punch: McGill

Pen: Zig Writer, EK Success

Computer font: Arial, Microsoft Word

Title: Karen got the idea from the *Toy Story* logo.

"Tweedle Dee and Tweedle Dum"

by Valerie Dellastatious
Orem, UT

SUPPLIES

Patterned paper: PrintWorks

Die cuts: Dayco

Diamond punch: Family Treasures

Computer font: CK Script, "The Best of Creative Lettering" CD Vol. 1, *Creating Keepsakes*

AUDREY, LAURIE, EMILEE, AMY & NIK GRIN
AS ROGER RABBIT GIVES A "HIGH FOUR"!

AMY POSES WITH HER NEW BOYFRIEND!
WHAT WILL JESSICA RABBIT SAY?

WHAT AN
OPPOR"TOON"ITY !
OUR TRIP TO DISNEYLAND
WAS A DREAM COME TRUE.
WE RENTED A VAN TO
MAKE THE TRIP IN OCTOBER
1989. EMILEE WAS A
SENIOR IN HIGH SCHOOL,
SO WE KNEW THIS WOULD
BE OUR LAST CHANCE TO BE
TOGETHER AS A FAMILY.
IT WAS THE HAPPIEST TWO
DAYS AT THE HAPPIEST
PLACE ON EARTH !

AMY CHECKS TO SEE IF
ROGER HAS A FUNNY BONE!

"What an Oppor'toon'ity!"

by Brenée Williams
Boise, ID
Photos by Jeanne English
Salt Lake City, UT
S U P P L I E S
Patterned paper:
The Paper Patch

Circle punches: CARL Mfg. (small);
Family Treasures (large)
Hole punch: Punchline, McGill
Pen: Micron Pigma, Sakura
Roger Rabbit clothes: Brenée's own
design

"Shiver Me Timbers, It's the Englishes"

by Sally Garrod
East Lansing, MI
Photos by Jeanne English
Salt Lake City, UT
S U P P L I E S
Pirate scroll template: Pirate
Party, Provo Craft (scanned
and enlarged)

Rope rub-ons: Provo Craft
Stickers: Stickopotamus
Computer font: DJ Knobbish,
Fontastic! Vol. 2, D.J. Inkers
Chalk: D.O.T.S.

"Shiver Me
Timbers,
It's the
English's!"

"Dad! Smee says I'm
his new treasure?" Amy
and Smee (left and
below with Nik).

"Smile Hook or Dad will run
you   through!"   Hook, Dad,
Audrey and Amy (above).

Smee and Nik (right), what a
crew.

Captain Hook next to Captain Hook
alias Nikolaus English (left).

Disneyland
October, 1989

Minnie and Heathy

Pinocchio

For my 25th birthday, I spent it at Disneyland with my mom, Brenda, Larry, Sara, Joyce and Brenda Butters. We had a blast there! We had a 3 Day Flex Pass which gave us plenty of time for the rides and to eat lots of popcorn, ice cream cotton candy and my favorite strawberry churros! I had so much fun and can't wait till next year!

Buzz, army guy and I at Tomorrow Land

Tigger and I after Splash Mountain!

Pooh and Eeyore at the corner

I love Mickey

Shopping with Goofy!

"Disney Friends"

by Heather McCurdy
Pebbles in my Pocket
Orem, UT
SUPPLIES
Lettering template: Block, ABC Tracers, EK Success
Punches: Family Treasures (circles); All Night Media (spiral)
Hole punches: Punchline, McGill
Paper doll: Paperkins, EK Success
Patterned paper (paper doll's shirt): Provo Craft
Pen: Zig Writer, EK Success

"If You Wish Upon a Star"

by Brenda Bennett
Morenci, AZ
Photos by Stacy Dill
Orem, UT
SUPPLIES
Patterned paper: Kangaroo & Joey Co.
Computer font (title): Doodle Summer, PagePrintables, Cock-A-Doodle Design Inc.
Vellum: The Paper Company
Pens: Pen-touch, Sakura (white); Zig Writer, EK Success (black)
Small star punch: Fiskars
Star template (medium and large stars): "Star" Micro Template, Provo Craft
Crystal ball: Brenda's own design

Jessica is a huge Disney fan. She has every movie memorized. She started from France in 1998 and her Aunt Stacy took her to see Disneyland! She was in heaven!

Jessica and all her favorite stars!

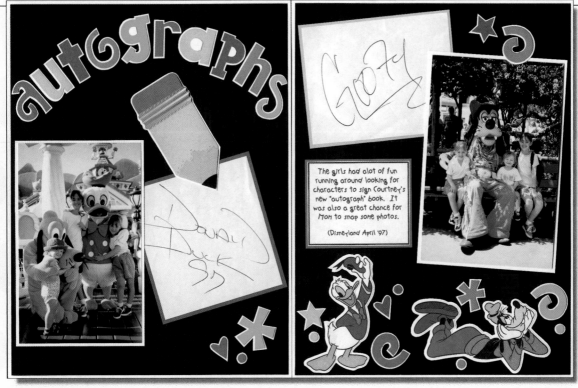

"Autographs"

by Brenda Cosgrove
Pebbles in my Pocket
Orem, UT
S U P P L I E S
Lettering template: Block and Funky,
ABC Tracers, EK Success; Block Serif
and Classic, Pebble Tracers,
Pebbles in my Pocket
Accents template: Funky, Theme
Stencils, Pebbles in my Pocket

Pencil die cut: Pebbles in my Pocket
Computer font: DJ Crazed, Fontastic!
Vol. 2, D.J. Inkers
Idea to note: Brenda used a Fiskars'
paper crimper to add dimension to the
"metal" portion of the pencil die cut.
Memorabilia idea: Brenda included
autographs from Disney characters
next to their pictures.

"Autographs"

by Michelle Snyder
Nampa, ID
S U P P L I E S
Pen: My Legacy Writer, Close To My Heart/D.O.T.S.
Mickey punch: All Night Media
Memorabilia idea: Michelle scanned the front of
the Disneyland autograph book and included it
with the autographs on the layout.

We just happened to spot Pinocchio in Italy at Epcot while we were waiting to be called for our table at Alfredo's. The kids were inside with their grandparents so we used our two way radios to call them out.

"Pinocchio"

by Grace T. Breeden
A Page In Time
Lincoln, NE
S U P P L I E S
Patterned paper: Keeping Memories Alive (background); Paper Adventures (polka dots); Frances Meyer (wood)
Photo frames: Frame-Ups, My Mind's Eye
Die-cut letters: DJ Daze, Accu-Cut Systems

Computer font: Scrap Hearts, Lettering Delights Vol. 1, Inspire Graphics
Scissors: Pinking edge, Fiskars
Circle punches: Family Treasures
Pen: Zig Millennium, EK Success
Pinocchio paper piecing: Grace's own design

"Pinocchio"

by Joyce Hill Schweitzer
Greensboro, NC
S U P P L I E S
Scissors: Deckle edge, Family Treasures
Pens: Tombow; Micron Pigma, Sakura; Zig Writer, EK Success
Heart and tears border punch: Family Treasures

Musical note stickers: Mrs. Grossman's
Idea to note: Joyce based her background drawings on the *Pinocchio* story by Collodi, a Walt Disney production.

WELCOME to Breakfast a la Disney hosted by PINOCCHIO

Take the straight and narrow path
And if you start to slide
Always let your conscience be your guide
And give a little whistle!

When you get in trouble
And you don't know right from wrong,
Give a little whistle!

When you meet temptation
And the urge is very strong,
Give a little whistle!

PLEASURE ISLAND

J. Worthington Foulfellow was such a handsome, beguiling fox. With Gideon, his scoundrel feline sidekick, they charmed us right out of our breakfasts.

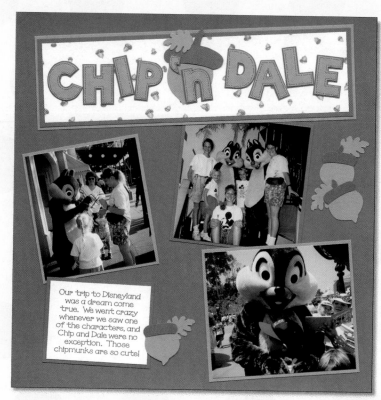

"Chip 'n Dale"
by Beth Wakulsky
Haslett, MI
Photos by Jeanne English
Salt Lake City, UT
SUPPLIES
Patterned paper: NRN Designs
Lettering template: Block, ABC Tracers, EK Success
Acorn die cuts: Ellison
Leaf punch: Emagination Crafts Inc.
Computer font: DJ Squared, Fontastic! Vol. 1, D.J. Inkers

"What a Group of Characters"
by Brenée Williams
Boise, ID
Photos by Peggy Peterson
Park City, UT
SUPPLIES
Lettering template: Alphabet, Close To My Heart/D.O.T.S.
Chalk: Craf-T Products
Pens: Zig Writer and Zig Opaque Writer, EK Success

Our trip to Disneyland was a dream come true. We went crazy whenever we saw one of the characters, and Chip and Dale were no exception. Those chipmunks are so cute!

We had a terrific trip to Disneyland. Jared was quite a character this trip.

His infectious laugh and quirky sense of humor made even the longest lines seem short!

Paper edge: Corkscrew by Fiskars

"Tarzan"
by Sandy Rowlette
Berea, KY
SUPPLIES
Patterned paper: PrintWorks
Leaves: Sandy scanned the leaves from
The Jungle Book published by Little Golden Book.
Tarzan characters: Sandy scanned the Tarzan
characters from a Life cereal box.
Tree: Sandy's own design
Computer font: Alleycat ICG, Pagemaker 6.5

"Say Cheese"
by Erin Terrell
San Antonio, TX
Photos by Dawn Leighter
Centerville, UT
SUPPLIES
Patterned paper: Colors By Design
Computer font (title): Disney Print, QuarkXPress
Pens: Zig Writers, EK Success
Chalk (shading on title blocks): Craf-T Products
Stars: Erin's own designs

OCT. 3
1997

We surprised Justine with a trip to Disneyland for her 6th birthday. She thought we were going to pick out a pinata, so when we showed up at the airport instead, she started to cry. "You mean everyone knew, but ME?" she asked. By the time we got to our gate, however, she was bouncing around and telling everyone, "It's my birthday! I'm going to Disneyland!"

We stayed at the Disneyland Hotel, dined with Mickey and Minnie, and posed with all the beautiful princesses. They gave June a Happy Birthday pin to wear, and everyone on the rides sang to her. Every night we stayed until the park closed. It was great. In the airplane on the way home, June said, "That was pretty fun, but next year can I just have a pinata instead?"

my birthday at

Disneyland

"My Birthday at Disneyland"

by Brandice Bringhurst
Layton, UT
SUPPLIES

Patterned paper: Provo Craft
Alphabet rubber stamps:
Stampin' Up!
Daisy die cuts: My Mind's Eye
Computer font: Architect,
PrintMaster Platinum

Idea to note: Brandice used a shopping bag from Disneyland as a template for her "Disneyland" letters. She then embossed the letters, cut them out and mounted them on the layout.

"What a Bunch of Characters"

by Erin Terrell
San Antonio, TX
Photos by Cindy Yip
San Diego, CA
SUPPLIES

Patterned paper: Keeping
Memories Alive
Lettering template: Scrapbook,
Provo Craft

Alphabet letters: "Scrapbook"
Alphabitties, Repositionable Sticky
Die-Cut Letters, Provo Craft
Computer font: DJ FiddleSticks,
FiddleSticks, D.J. Inkers
Pen: Gelly Roll, Sakura
Stars: Erin's own designs

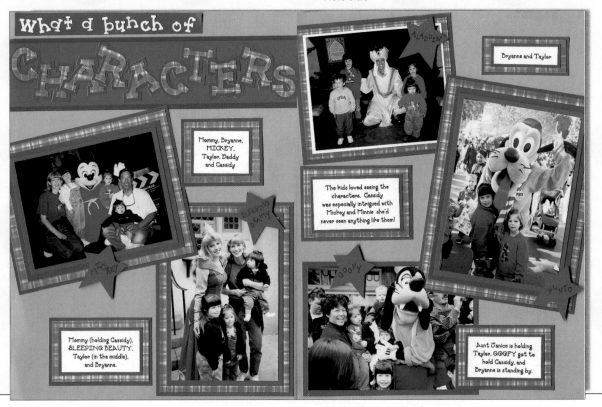

What a bunch of

CHARACTERS

ALADDIN

Bryanne and Taylor

Mommy, Bryanne, MICKEY, Taylor, Daddy and Cassidy

The kids loved seeing the characters. Cassidy was especially intrigued with Mickey and Minnie, she'd never seen anything like them!

PLUTO

MICKEY

SLEEPING BEAUTY

GOOFY

Mommy (holding Cassidy), SLEEPING BEAUTY, Taylor (in the middle), and Bryanne.

Aunt Janice is holding Taylor, GOOFY got to hold Cassidy, and Bryanne is standing by.

by Becky Higgins

Try Our Three "All Ears" Alphabets

We've made it fun and easy. Why? Because we like you!

As you devour every page of *The Big Idea Book of Disney Memories,* I know you're making lots of mental notes—and maybe even some sketches—of ideas for your pages. This creative brainstorming phase is almost as fun as the scrapbooking process itself! As your inspirations begin to materialize, keep in mind the role that lettering plays in achieving a truly magical look for your layouts. These suggestions will make it as easy as ABC!

Just as everyone has a unique experience at "the Happiest Place on Earth," everyone also has a distinctively personal scrapbooking approach. So here are *three* creative lettering styles from which to choose. And if you take away the accents, you'll have three *more* alphabets to add to your collection of versatile favorites.

STYLE #1

These playful, stocky letters are easier to create than it looks. Simply draw your title lightly in pencil, spacing the letters so there's room for adding bulk to each

HOT TIP:
You can use these styles on practically any scrapbook page. Depending on your theme, you can replace the mouse ears with hearts, stars, flowers—or nothing at all!

Figure 1. Use three colors that complement your photographs when coloring in the boxes of Style #2. *Photos by Alyssa Allgaier and pages by Becky Higgins*. **Supplies** *Club Disney house:* cut from a brochure; *Vellum:* Paper Adventures; *Colored pencils:* Prismacolor, Sanford.

STYLE #1

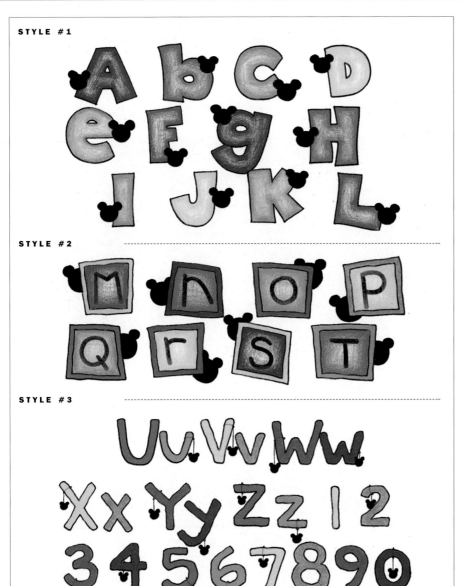

STYLE #2

STYLE #3

Figure 1) or four (see sample, "Walt Disney World" on page 52) works nicely. Try shading the inside box with the same technique as Style #1: Color darker toward the outer edge and go lighter toward the middle.

STYLE #3
The style at the bottom of the alphabet is daintier and more subtle than most, but the dangling mouse ears make this look adorable for almost any Disney-themed page. Use the tips mentioned in Style #1 to create the block-style lettering, but instead of spacing out your letters, keep these slender ones close together. I prefer to draw my outlines a little crooked for a less formal, more juvenile and playful look, but you can keep them straight as a variation. Use a very fine-point pen for the "strings" from which the mouse ears dangle.

LETTERING TIPS
◆ Drawing the little mouse ears motifs is as easy as drawing a black circle with two smaller black circles on top for his ears.
◆ If you add mouse ears motifs to your titles, you don't need to put one on every letter. It might look too crowded or too uniform if you go overboard. Check out the title in Figure 3 and the "Memories" and "Mouseketeers™" samples on page 52.
◆ The most important thing to remember when you're coloring your titles is that the hues should complement your pictures and your theme. Brights may be appropriate for most pages, but don't forget about your other, softer options (see "Mouseketeers™").
◆ To unify your layouts and give them a nice flow, try using one style of lettering for all of your section headings. This will add a charming storybook quality to your vacation layouts.

Figure 2. *Alphabet by Becky Higgins*. **Supplies** *Black pen: Zig Writer, EK Success; Colored pencils: Prismacolor, Sanford.*

one. Then draw parallel lines along each part of each letter, just as you would for any block-style format. Before going over these outlines with a permanent pen, be sure to widen some of the ends for a less-formal look. After outlining each letter, add small mouse ears randomly, then color the letters. Pens are great, or you can try your hand at colored pencils as shown in the alphabet (see Figure 2). Simply shade heavier and darker around the edges, and fade it out (apply less pressure) as you color toward the center.

STYLE #2
Drawing uneven blocks to frame each letter can add a simple yet stunning touch to any scrapbook page—especially your Disney-themed layouts, if you add the little mouse ears peeking from behind the boxes. Draw trapezoid-shape boxes with uneven lines, and then draw another line inside each box. Now draw a letter within each box; I prefer keeping the letters quite simple, because the boxes are plenty eye-catching. It's fun to use a different color for each box and each outside border. A scheme of three colors (see

◆ If you want your letters to "pop" off the page, add a drop-shadow effect by using a light gray pen and drawing around the bottom and left parts of each letter (or the top and right, or whatever).

There you have it—three new lettering styles for your Disney-themed scrapbook pages—and for your other pages as well! Remember always to draw with a pencil first, and if you're not achieving the desired look, you can always get out the old light box and trace these letters. No matter how you get the finished results, these three lettering styles are sure to provide fanciful embellishments to your pages. And throughout this book, you'll find lots of complementary layouts that will help you capture the spirit of Disney. ♥

Figure 3. Style #3 is especially great when space is limited. Dangle mouse ears here and there, but don't feel obligated to have one hanging from every letter! *Photos by Lanae Johnson and page by Becky Higgins*. **Supplies** *Vellum:* Paper Adventures; *Mickey and Minnie:* cut from brochure; *Circle punch:* McGill; *Black photo corners:* 3L Corp. *Idea to note:* Becky triple-layered the vellum to ensure that the title is legible with the busy dots behind.

Figure 4. Make your lettering "pop" off the page by adding a subtle gray shadow. *Photos by Stacy Dill and page by Becky Higgins*. **Supplies** *Rub-on character:* Hot Off the Press; *Pens:* Zig Writers, EK Success; *Colored pencils and colorless blending pencil:* Prismacolor, Sanford.

Figure 5. *Samples by Becky Higgins*. **Supplies** *Pens:* Zig Writer, EK Success and Artist, Marvy Uchida; *Colored pencils and colorless blending pencil:* Prismacolor, Sanford; *Diamond Dust paper (on "Walt Disney World"):* Paper Adventures.

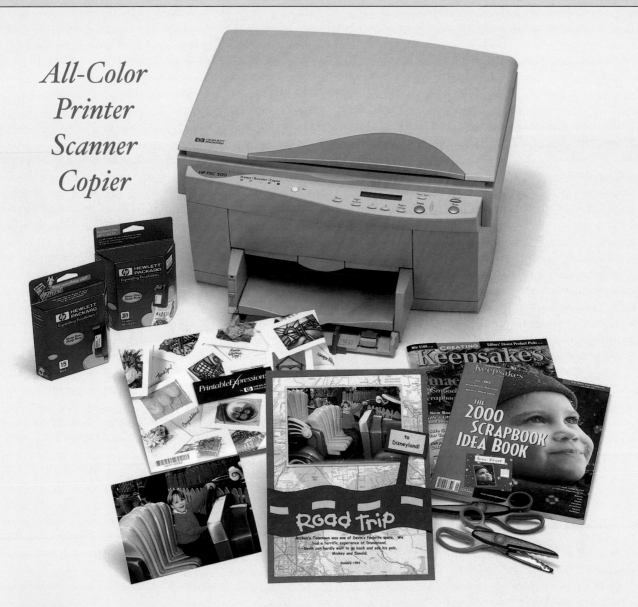

All-Color Printer Scanner Copier

There's no doubt about it—we're smack in the middle of the information age. So put some high technology into your scrapbooking arsenal with Hewlett-Packard Company's PSC 500 All-color Printer/Scanner/Copier and your personal computer.

Check out these fun uses:

- Scan memorabilia too large to include in your scrapbook (such as sections of blankets or clothing) and include the scanned item in your scrapbook
- Use the flatbed scanner to scan 3-D items that complement your layout theme and make your own patterned paper (maps, see above, flowers and jelly beans are just a few ideas)
- Scan stamped images or clip art and enlarge or shrink so that the items are proportional to your layout
- Electronically alter photos (including enlarging, reducing, cropping or enhancing colors)
- Make copies of family layouts and include them in grandparents' or kids' albums without using a PC
- "Freshen up" old, faded photos by scanning and printing them onto HP photo paper
- E-mail photos to family and friends

The PSC 500 features easy-to-use software that helps you complete photo projects in minutes. Everything you print, scan or copy on the HP PSC 500 will look true to the original, complete with vivid colors.

HEWLETT-PACKARD COMPANY

Phone: 800/752-0900

Web site: . . . . *www.hp.com/go/all-in-one*

MSRP:

HP PSC 500: $399.00

Available at computer and consumer electronics stores.

OUR TRIP TO

DISNEYLAND

We LOVE Disney!

There is no doubt—
Disneyland really is
"the 'Happiest Place
on Earth.'" Brandon
and I loved every
moment of our Disney
trip. We had so much
fun meeting our
favorite characters—
I think we met every
single one!

Layout by: Brenda Bennett; Photos by: Emilee Riley; Disney characters © Disney Enterprises, Inc.

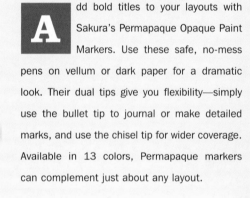

*A Full Line
of Archival
Pens*

Add bold titles to your layouts with Sakura's Permapaque Opaque Paint Markers. Use these safe, no-mess pens on vellum or dark paper for a dramatic look. Their dual tips give you flexibility—simply use the bullet tip to journal or make detailed marks, and use the chisel tip for wider coverage. Available in 13 colors, Permapaque markers can complement just about any layout.

• • •

Check out Sakura's complete line of archival pens. They can fill all your scrapbooking needs, from elegant calligraphy to lighthearted doodling.

SAKURA OF AMERICA

Web site: . . . . *www.gellyroll.com*

MSRP:

Permapaque® $2.50

Gelly Roll® $1.29

Pigma Color Technology/Micron® $2.69

PIONEER® FAMILY TREASURES® DELUXE E-Z LOAD® MEMORY BOOKS

Acid Free and Photo Safe

Just because you've adhered your final photo doesn't mean that your layout is complete. Store your precious memories in Pioneer® Family Treasures® Deluxe E-Z Load® Memory Books. This acid- and lignin-free product contains no PVC and has received *Creating Keepsakes'* CK OK seal of approval.

Deluxe E-Z Load® Memory Books are available in four popular sizes—8½" x 11", 12" x 12", 5" x 7" and 12" x 15"—and come with 10 top-loading page protectors and 10 sheets of heavy white paper. The albums are made with washable padded fabric covers and have rounded spines and corners, and the reinforced post binding (which can be expanded to accommodate unlimited black or white refills) allows the pages in the album to lie flat. The top-loading page protectors allow you to slip layouts in and out easily. (Refill pages fit post-bound, three-ring and staple-strap style memory books.)

Don't forget to look for these other acid-free and photo-safe products available from Pioneer®: clear, black, rainbow or metallic photo corners, photo mounts, mounting tape and glue sticks, photo caption stickers and 3-D gold letters, gel ink pens, craft scissors, photo templates, colored paper and three-ring binders.

PIONEER PHOTO ALBUMS INC.

Phone: 800/366-3686

Web site: . . . . *www.pioneerphotoalbums.com*

E-mail: . . . . . . *pioneer@pioneerphotoalbums.com*

PIONEER
Photo Albums

Pop 'n Swap Cutouts

Pop 'n Swap Cutouts—use the giant die cuts on one layout and the pop-out shapes for a second page!

If you're like most visitors to "the Happiest Place on Earth™," you probably returned home with a stash of photos just begging to be placed in a scrapbook. The new Pop 'n Swap 12" x 12" Cutouts by Times to Cherish by Current will make it happen in a snap. Our large 12" x 12" die cuts will help you instantly design entire pages. Just pop out the interior shapes, and you have a collage of frames for your photos. Then "swap" and use the die-cut shapes to create a coordinated second page! Each set contains nine sheets in nine colors; three designs. Times to Cherish by Current is the headquarters for your scrapbooking needs. We have our own line of paper, stickers and accessories, which will help you make your scrapbook truly one of a kind. Naturally, our products are acid free and photograph friendly.

We're always introducing new products—so visit our web site at *www.timestocherish.com*. We're striving to make scrapbooking your memories fun *and* affordable.

TIMES TO CHERISH BY CURRENT

Phone: 800/848-2848

MSRP:

Pop 'n Swap Cutouts . . $5.99

Have you ever found yourself looking for a sticker, but you couldn't find just the right one? Therm O Web has a solution for you. Keep a Memory™ Mounting Adhesive will turn any item—from stamped images to clip art and from stationery to punched items—into a sticker!

For example, simply place a strip of paper on a sheet of Mounting Adhesive, then punch out your desired shape. Voilá, you've made your own sticker—without gumming up your punch. Keep a Memory™ Mounting Adhesive is repositionable for up to 24 hours, so if you're not quite satisfied with how the elements are arranged, you can move them around until you've achieved your desired look. Then, lightly rub the object with your finger, which makes the adhesive permanent.

Don't forget Keep a Memory™ Mounting Tape. This double-sided tape is temporarily repositionable and is perfect when adhering paper, photos or mats to your layout.

THERM O WEB

Phone: 800/323-0799

Web site: . . . . *www.thermoweb.com*

MSRP:

Keep a Memory™ Mounting Adhesive . . . .
. . . . $3.29–$5.45

Keep a Memory™ Mounting Tape . . $2.93

Layout by: Kerri Bradford; Photos by: Peggy Peterson; Disney characters © Disney Enterprises, Inc.

Mounting Adhesives

Therm O Web

"Kids" Stickers and Borders

It's hard to visit "the Happiest Place on Earth™" without taking a ton of photos. Me & my BIG ideas offers the perfect companion to your photos—theme-park "kids" stickers and borders can help you make unforgettable scrapbook pages!

Of course, these new stickers will mix and match perfectly with the other stickers and patterned paper in the me & my BIG ideas line.

Use the stickers on their own to make quick and easy layouts. Or, cut the stickers apart to make more complex layouts. For example, the border stickers will make terrific picture frames—or highlight a photo by having a sticker "kid" peek from behind it. The possibilities are limited only by your imagination.

Scrapbooking has never been easier (or had so much personality!).

ME & MY BIG IDEAS

Address: . . . . 23091 Antonio Parkway #320
. . . . Rancho Santa Margarita, CA 92688
Web site: . . . . *www.meandmybigideas.com*
. . . . (wholesale only)

Layout by: Brendee Williams; Photos by: Natalie Cuglietta; Disney characters © Disney Enterprises, Inc.

Terrific Templates

PUZZLE MATES

Phone: 888/595-2887

Web site: . . . . *www.puzzlemates.com*

MSRP:

Puzzle Mates templates $8.99

Puzzle Mates Puzzle Template Books $12.99

Endless Oval Idea Book $9.99

Magic Matter $11.99

Use the Puzzle Mates templates to transform your precious photos into magical layouts! Design your layouts in three easy steps:

❶ Select your photos. You can use as many as seven photos with the Puzzle Mates template.

❷ Place the template over your photos, and use a grease pencil to trace the shapes onto your photos.

❸ Arrange the photos on your layout and embellish as desired.

Whether you have a few minutes or a few hours to work on your layout, the Puzzle Mates template system will make scrapbooking a snap. Your designs can incorporate the classic Puzzle Mates style, or you can take a few minutes to rearrange the shapes and make unique designs that complement your layout's theme. (*Hint:* If you're making unique designs, cut the template shapes out of paper first, and rearrange until you're satisfied.) And don't worry about the size of the templates—the Puzzle Mates Original Extension Strips on the templates allow you to make layouts for any album size.

Magical Memories...

From Toontown® to Tomorrowland®, from meeting Mickey Mouse to surviving Splash Mountain™, you can preserve your special memories with Close To My Heart® rubber stamp designs and exclusive scrapbook products. You'll open a magical new world with our premium Exclusive Inks® markers and stamp pads which match our Background and Texture Papers—in over 64 distinctive colors. Close To My Heart products and idea books will inspire you to create your best work. Whether you're interested in getting new ideas, purchasing exclusive products, hosting a home demonstration, or learning more about the Close To My Heart business opportunity, give us a call today!

Close to my Heart

1-888-655-6552

www.dotadventures.com

HOT SPOTS

Welcome to
BIG THUNDER
THE BIGGEST
LITTLE BOOM TOWN

CHELSIE & LAINE
DISNEYLAND 1999

Vacation Tip

If your kids need to release some energy,

head over to *Tarzan's Treehouse*,

Tom Sawyer Island or *Goofy's Bounce*

House in Mickey's Toontown.

"Welcome to Big Thunder Mountain Railroad™"

by Laurie Carley
Centralia, WA
SUPPLIES

Wood patterned paper: Paper Pizazz, Hot Off The Press
Train: Laurie's own design
Chalks: Craf-T Products
Computer font: Stagecoach, Print Shop Deluxe
Pen: Metallic Gel Pen, Marvy Uchida

"Frontierland®"

by Lori Bergmann

Turlock, CA

SUPPLIES

Punches: All Night Media

Patterned paper: Provo Craft (asphalt); Lori's own design (wood)

Pens: Micron Pigma, Sakura; Zig Writer, EK Success

Colored pencils: Prismacolor, Sanford

Chalk: Stampin' Up!

Entrance gate: Lori's own design

"Big Thunder Mountain Railroad™"

by Julie Anderson

Renton, WA

SUPPLIES

Lettering template: Rustic Letters, Frances Meyer

Train die cut: Ellison

Scissors: Deckle edge, Fiskars

Pens: Zig Writers, EK Success

Cacti, train track, snake and hat: Julie's own designs

"Big Thunder Mountain Railroad™*"*

by Shauna Wright
Salt Lake City, UT

S U P P L I E S

Die cuts: Ellison

Scissors: Deckle edge, Fiskars

Pen: Zig Writer, EK Success

Travis loves trains, so it's no wonder that this was one of his favorite rides.

Big Thunder Mountain Railroad

Big Thunder Mountain Railroad

Kristie, Brittany, and Shell

Big Thunder Mountain Railroad is one of our favorites rides at Disneyland

"Big Thunder"

Shelly Patten
Pebbles in my Pocket
Orem, UT

S U P P L I E S

Lettering template: Log Cabin, ABC Tracers, EK Success

Pen: Zig Writer, EK Success

Mountains, train tracks and trees: Shelly's own designs

"Tom Sawyer Island™*"*

by Desirée Tanner
Provo Craft
Provo, UT

S U P P L I E S

Patterned paper: Provo Craft

Rope rub-ons: Tied Up in Knots, Provo Craft

Children and canoes accents: On the Go, Dress-Ups, Provo Craft

Tree punch: Long Reach Art Punch, McGill

Larger trees: Desirée's own designs

Pen: Zig Writer, EK Success

We love to paddle over to the island and play on the rocks and rope bridges.

Tom Sawyer's Island

Summer 1993

Paper edge: Corkscrew by Fiskars

"Adventureland®"

by Janet Meyerhoffer

Ogden, UT

SUPPLIES

Rubber stamps: Festive Fun Caps, Close To My Heart/D.O.T.S.

Spear stationery: Sonburn

Computer font: DJ Curl, Fontastic! Vol. 2, D.J. Inkers

"Adventureland®"

by Lori Bergmann

Turlock, CA

SUPPLIES

Mickey punch: All Night Media

Pens: Micron Pigma, Sakura; Zig Writer, EK Success

Chalk: Stampin' Up!

Other: Lori used raffia and floss to make the title enhancements.

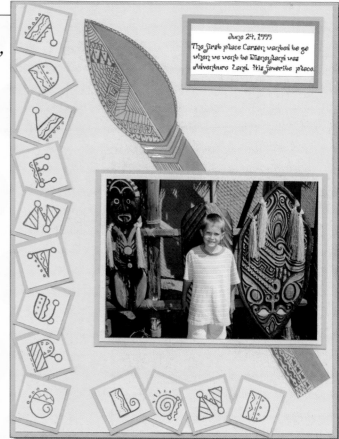

June 24, 1999
The first place Carson wanted to go when we went to Disneyland was Adventure Land. His favorite place.

We enjoyed a thrilling, but corny, ride through the jungle — the girls were never quite sure if the animals were real or not! We didn't know it yet, but this was the Swiss Family's last year in existance — It was replaced with Tarzan's Treehouse in 1999. Mommy & Daddy loved the new Indiana Jones Adventure ride!

the girls thought Aladdin was a cutie — Mommy & Nana thought so too!

NEW! Disneyland TARZAN'S TREEHOUSE

In July of 1999 Jenny and I explored Tarzan's home.

We met Jane, who was very gracious!

We had so much fun swinging from the branches

Tarzan himself swung by to say "hello"

We overlooked the tree tops!

It was quite an adventure and all we have to say is...

It's A Jungle Up There!

AUTOPIA 15 SPEED LIMIT

Paper edge: Corkscrew by Fiskars

"Tarzan's Treehouse™"
by Kelley Morrison
Elk Grove, CA
SUPPLIES
Leaf die cuts: Ellison
Scissors: Deckle edge, Fiskars
Pens: Zig Memory System, EK Success
Tree: Kelley's own design
Idea to note: Kelley took photos of the Tarzan story as it progressed throughout *Tarzan's Treehouse* and included them on the layout. She also included the *Tarzan's Treehouse* logo from a Disneyland brochure.

"Autopia"
by Kim Heffington
Puzzle Mates
Brea, CA
SUPPLIES
Number template: Puzzle Template Book Vol. 2, Numbers & Celebrations, Puzzle Mates
Lettering template: Classic, Pebble Tracers, Pebbles in my Pocket

Photo tip:
Get photos of group members next to the entrance signs into each kingdom, park, land or other main attraction.

THIS PAGE IS DEDICATED TO MY SHELBY.

"It's a Small World™"

by Nicolle Perez
Las Vegas, NV
SUPPLIES
Lettering template: Dot Letters, Frances Meyer
Punches: Marvy Uchida (snowflake and small bow); Family Treasures (circle, balloon, small and large daisies, large bow and scallop)
Star, small flower and hole punches: Punchline, McGill
Photo sleeves: Lineco
Pens: Zig Writer, EK Success; Milky Gel Roller, Pentel
Flags and paper dolls: Nicolle's own designs
Idea to note: Nicolle used photo sleeves to include a lot of photos on one layout.

"It's a Small World™"

by Shelly Patten
Pebbles in my Pocket
Orem, UT
SUPPLIES
Embossed paper: Penny Black
Pen: Zig Writer, EK Success
Lettering idea: Shelly's own design

Brittany, Shelly, Jessica and Kristie

just mad about disneyland

Jessica was not sure she wanted to ride in this big teacup!

Jessica and Mom
The next day Jessie decided that she did like the teacup ride as long as Mom didn't spin the cup too fast.
Disneyland 1995

Fantasyland is the BEST!

Jordan & Grandma Chris on the Teacups.

Jordan could not wait to go on the Dumbo ride!

M Y F A V O R I T E S

"Just Mad about Disneyland"
by Susan Nelson
Orem, UT
SUPPLIES
Alphabet stamps: Hero Arts
Colored pencils: Memory Pencils, EK Success
Pen: Zig Writer, EK Success
Paper piecing: Susan's own designs

"My Favorites"
by Kerri Bradford
Orem, UT
SUPPLIES
Patterned paper: MM's Design
(pink polka dot and green plaid);
Colors By Design (pink checked)
Flower enhancements: Corner &
Border Stickers, Provo Craft
Tea cup: Kerri's own design
Paper doll and clothes:
Dress Ups, Provo Craft
Spiral punch: All Night Media
Alphabet letters: "Fat Dot"
Alphabitties, Repositionable Sticky
Die-Cut Letters, Provo Craft
Pen: Zig Writer, EK Success

Paper edge: Corkscrew by Fiskars

"The Sword in the Stone"

by Desirée Tanner
Provo Craft
Provo, UT

SUPPLIES

Patterned paper: Wishes and Dreams,
Scrap Pads, Provo Craft
Pens: Zig Writers, EK Success
Paper doll template: Coluzzle, Provo Craft

PHOTO OP:

Take photos of you and other members in your
group attempting to pull the sword out of the stone,
which is behind *Sleeping Beauty Castle.*

Page titles could include: "'Foil'ed Again" or
"Who Said the Pen Is Mightier than the Sword?"

"Goofy's Bounce House"

by Kerri Bradford
Orem, UT

SUPPLIES

Patterned paper: Bo-Bunny Press (plaid); Keeping Memories Alive (yellow)
Goofy stationery: Paper Pizazz, Hot Off The Press
Alphabet letters: "Funky" (large) and "Scrapbook" Alphabitties (small),
Repositionable Sticky Die-Cut Letters, Provo Craft
Girl sticker: me & my BIG ideas
Scissors (doily on chair): Scallop edge, Fiskars
Pen: Zig Writer, EK Success
Chair: Kerri's own design

"Toontown®"

by Jana Francis
Provo, UT
Photo by Peggy Peterson
Park City, UT

SUPPLIES

Patterned paper: Colors By Design

Pens: Zig Writers, EK Success
Computer font: CK Toggle,
"The Best of Creative Lettering"
CD Vol. 2, *Creating Keepsakes*
Lettering and fish paper piecing:
Jana's own design

Kassidy & Zach with their pal, Minnie.

WHERE'S THE FIRE?!!

DOG POUND

SOMEBODY GET US OUT OF HERE!

Everyone wave Hello!

KNOCK, KNOCK. Nobody's Home.

Waiting for the Roger Rabbit ride.

TNT

TOONTOWN

"Mickey's Toontown®"
by Kerri Bradford
Orem, UT
SUPPLIES

Patterned paper: Provo Craft (blue and wood);
Scrap Pads, Provo Craft (green hills, blue
with yellow stars, and green with black
polka dots); Robin's Nest (red stripe)
Mickey and Pluto stationery:
Paper Pizazz, Hot Off The Press
Punches: All Night Media (spiral); Marvy
Uchida (circle); McGill (teardrop on sun)
Scissors: Pinking and Zipper edges, Provo Craft
Brick and stone border stickers: Mrs. Grossman's
Pens: Zig Writer, EK Success; Milky Gel Roller, Pentel
Sun, clouds, crate and bone: Kerri's own designs
Jolley Trolley, house, fireworks, TNT and light: Kerri got
the ideas from a Disneyland souvenir book.

"Mickey's Toontown®"
by Missy Jaycox
St. Louis, MO
SUPPLIES

Rubber stamps: Brush Stroke, D.O.T.S. (alphabet
letters); Delta Technical Coatings (Mickey shorts,
gloves, shoes and ears)
Ink pad: Close To My Heart/D.O.T.S.
Acrylic paint (on Mickey stamps): Apple Barrel
Computer font: Disney Print, QuarkXPress

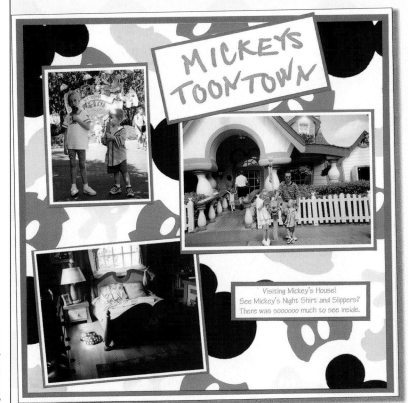

MICKEYS TOONTOWN

Visiting Mickey's House!
See Mickey's Night Shirt and Slippers?
There was sooooooo much to see inside.

Paper edge: Corkscrew by Fiskars

"Minnie's House"

by Karen Petersen
Mom and Me Scrapbooking
Salt Lake City, UT
Photos by Laurie Green
Alpine, UT
S U P P L I E S

Patterned paper: Paper Adventures
Die cuts: Ellison (clouds, sun and mailbox);
Pebbles in my Pocket (grass border); Accu-Cut Systems
(gingerbread house)
Punches: Family Treasures
Computer font: Scrap Simple, Lettering
Delights Vol. 1, Inspire Graphics

"Minnie's House"

by Ellen James
Orem, UT
S U P P L I E S
Patterned paper: Source unknown
Minnie Mouse stationery: Paper Pizazz,
Hot Off The Press
Mickey punch: All Night Media
Chalk: Craf-T Products
Pen: Zig Writer, EK Success

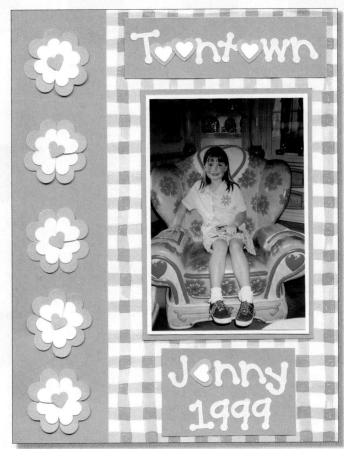

"Toontown®"
by Valerie Dellastatious
Orem, UT
SUPPLIES
Patterned paper: Jenny Faw Designs Inc.
Alphabet letters: "Fat Dot," Repositionable
Sticky Die-Cut Letters, Provo Craft
Heart punches: Marvy Uchida (small);
CARL Mfg. (medium); McGill (large)

"Visiting Minnie's House"
by Joan Wadsworth
Sandy, UT
Photos by Cindy Yip
San Diego, CA
SUPPLIES
Heart punch (cut in half for leaves): Marvy Uchida
Colored pencils: Mongol Water Coloring Pencils
Pen: Zig Writer, EK Success
Curtains and bows: Joan's own designs

The whole gang got to visit with Minnie Mouse. The girls just loved her fun house!

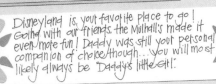

Disneyland is your favorite place to go! Going with our friends, the Mulhall's made it even more fun! Daddy was still your personal companion of choice though... you will most likely always be Daddy's little girl!

Paper edge: Corkscrew by Fiskars

"E-Ticket Night"

by Michelle Gillette
St. Peters, MO

SUPPLIES

Flower punch: All Night Media
Chalk: Craf-T Products
Pen: Milky Gel Roller, Pentel
Alphabet letter: Michelle's own design

"Astro Orbiter™"

by Amber Blakesley
Provo, UT

Photos by Laurie Green
Alpine, UT

SUPPLIES

Diamond Dust paper: Paper Adventures
Lettering template: Block, ABC Tracers, EK Success
Circle punches: Family Treasures

My favorite ride is definitely Space Mountain. Because the lines weren't too long, we were able to ride it several times.

Walt Disney World
October 1999

"Takin' Off for Tomorrowland®"

by Heather Thatcher
Draper, UT
Photos by Valerie Dellastatious
Orem, UT
S U P P L I E S
Patterned paper: Paperbilities, MPR
Marbled vellum: CTI Paper USA Inc.
Triangle punch: Family Treasures

Pens: Milky Gel Roller, Pentel;
Zig Writers, EK Success
Computer fonts: CK Anything Goes,
"The Best of Creative Lettering" CD
Vol. 1 and CK Toggle, "The Best of
Creative Lettering" CD Vol. 2, *Creating
Keepsakes*
Suns and exhaust: Heather's own
designs

"Blast Off into Tomorrowland®"

by Nancy Church
Augusta, GA
Photos by Dawn Leighter
Centerville, UT
S U P P L I E S
Star punches: Family Treasures
Computer font: Scrap Caps,
Lettering Delights Vol. 3,
Inspire Graphics

Astro Orbiter and planet:
Nancy's own designs
Idea to note: Nancy used
the letter "U" from a lettering
template to make the ring
around the planet.

Paper edge: Corkscrew by Fiskars

"A Pirate Voyage"

by Marcella Casebolt
Fremont, CA

SUPPLIES

Lettering template: Wacky Letters, Frances Meyer
Paper dolls: Accu-Cut Systems
Patterned paper: Paper Adventures (red plaid, blue
with white polka dots); Close To My Heart/D.O.T.S. (blue plaid)
Pens: Micron Pigma, Sakura; Milky Gel Roller, Pentel

"Pirates of the Caribbean™"

by Valerie Dellastatious
Orem, UT

SUPPLIES

Paper doll and clothes: Stamping Station
Treasure chest die cut: Ellison
Circle and swirl border punches (hair):
Family Treasures
Hole punches: Punchline, McGill
Computer font: Doodle Tipsy,
PagePrintables, Cock-A-Doodle Design Inc.

"Haunted Mansion™"
by Pam Talluto
Rochester Hills, MI
S U P P L I E S
Mulberry paper: Personal Stamp Exchange
Scissors: Deckle edge, Fiskars
Pen: Zig Writer, EK Success
Computer font: Accent Spooky,
downloaded from the Internet

"Main Street U.S.A."
by Jennifer Jensen
Hurricane, UT
Photos by Valerie Dellastatious
Orem, UT
S U P P L I E S
Patterned paper (green plaid): Northern Spy
Punches: Family Treasures
Pens: Zig Writer, EK Success; Gelly Roll, Sakura
Idea to note: Jennifer designed the "Main Street"
on the layout to match the one in the photos.

Paper edge: Corkscrew by Fiskars

"Disneyland Magical Memories"

by Carrie Duwelius
Aurora, IL

SUPPLIES

Patterned paper: Frances Meyer

Metallic paper: Making Memories

Castle template: Binding Memories

Colored vellum: Paper Adventures

Pens: Zig Millennium, EK Success; Pen-touch, Sakura (silver)

"Ariel's Grotto™"

by Nancy Church
Augusta, GA
Photos by Dawn Leighter
Centerville, UT

SUPPLIES

Patterned paper: Colors By Design

Alphabet letters: Pebbles ABC Stickers, Pebbles in my Pocket

Templates: Christmas, Theme Stencils, Pebbles in my Pocket (wave border); Funky, Provo Craft (splats)

Computer font: DJ Jumble, Scraps & Stitches, D.J. Inkers

"We Survived"

by Heather Spurlock
Salt Lake City, UT
S U P P L I E S
Lettering template: Block Serif, Pebble
Tracers, Pebbles in my Pocket
Vultures: Cut from the original mat that
came with her Splash Mountain photo
from Disneyland.

Corner edger: Art Deco, Fiskars
Colored pencils: Prismacolor, Sanford
Pen: Zig Writer, EK Success
Water splash and brier bush: Heather's
own designs.
Idea to note: Heather used double-
sided sponge tape to add dimension to
the vultures.

"Splash Mountain™*"*

by Lynsey Morris
Boise, ID
S U P P L I E S
Paper dolls: Stick Kids, Stamping Station
Grass die cut: Carolee's Creations
Chalk: Craf-T Products
Pens: Zig Writers, EK Success
Log and thorns: Lynsey's own designs

"Rides"

by Alycia Alvarez
Altus, OK
Photos by Cindy Yip
San Diego, CA
SUPPLIES
Patterned paper: Provo Craft
Diamond Dust paper: Paper Adventures
Lettering template: Fat Caps, Frances Meyer
Circle punch: Family Treasures

Computer font: CK Toggle, "The Best of Creative Lettering" CD Vol. 2, *Creating Keepsakes*
Pen: Zig Millennium, EK Success
Roller coaster: Alycia's own design
Other: Alycia "suspended" the sky-ride enhancement with string.
Idea to note: Alycia color copied and enlarged stickers from me & my BIG ideas to create the accents.

PHOTO OP

Before your carriage turns back into a pumpkin, have each person pose for a photo next to his or her favorite attraction. When the time comes to scrapbook these photos, your journaling should include the attraction's name, where it's located (what land or park), how many times the person rode it and why it's his or her favorite adventure. You may even want to make this photo op a tradition—each trip back, take another photo of the same person in the same spot.

Disneyland VACATION

Here's Jaena enjoying a ride on Dumbo The Flying Elephant in Fantasyland.

Vacation Tip

To get a good photo of a ride on *Dumbo the Flying Elephant,*
have the photographer "fly" in the elephant in front of you.
He or she can then turn around and capture the flight.

"Disneyland Vacation"
by Lanae Beth Johnson
Glendale, AZ
S U P P L I E S
Balloon die cuts: Accu-Cut Systems
Letter stickers: Frances Meyer
Pen: Micron Pigma, Sakura

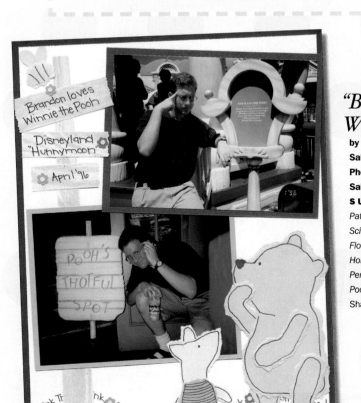

Brandon loves Winnie the Pooh

Disneyland "Hunnymoon"

April '96

POOH'S THOTFUL SPOT

Think Think Oh Bother! Think Oh Bother!

"Brandon Loves
Winnie the Pooh"
by Shannon Wolz
Salt Lake City, UT
Photos by Emilee Riley
Salt Lake City, UT
S U P P L I E S
Patterned paper: Provo Craft
Scissors: Deckle edge, Provo Craft
Flower punch: Punchline, McGill
Hole punch: Gemline, McGill
Pen: Zig Writer, EK Success
Pooh, Piglet, sign and bee:
Shannon's own designs

Paper edge: Corkscrew by Fiskars

"Disney MGM Studios"

by Barb Erickson
Colorado Springs, CO

SUPPLIES

Patterned paper: The Paper Patch
Border punch: All Night Media
Pen: Zig Writer, EK Success
Sticker: Disney
Clip art: From *Learn to Draw Mickey and Minnie* by Walter Foster

"Animation Academy Graduate"

by Noël Fields
North Branford, CT

SUPPLIES

Patterned paper: Paper Pizazz, Hot Off The Press
Mickey, Minnie and Donald Duck accents: Punch-Outs, Hot Off The Press
Punches: Marvy Uchida (sun); All Night Media (Mickey)

Corner edger: Regal, Fiskars
Embossing powder: Stamp Craft
Ultra-Fine Silver Jewel Glitter: Mark Enterprises
Pens: Zig Writer and Zig Opaque Writer, EK Success
Mickey Mouse sticker: Purchased at Walt Disney World

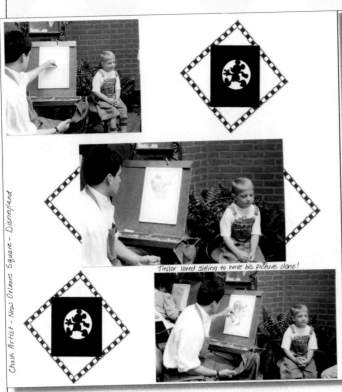

Chalk Artist - New Orleans Square - Disneyland

Taylor loved sitting to have his picture done!

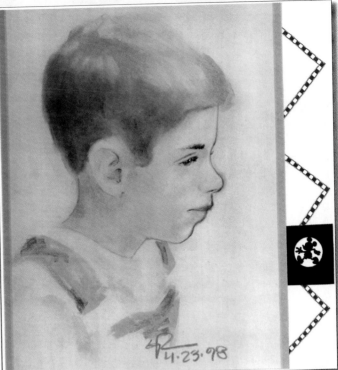

Paper edge: Corkscrew by Fiskars

"Chalk Artist"

by Amy Moor
Redmond, OR
S U P P L I E S

Rubber-stamp frame: Annette Adam Watkins
Ink pad: ColorBox, Clearsnap Inc.
Mickey Mouse punch: All Night Media
Pen: Zig Writer, EK Success
Memorabilia idea: Amy included
"work-in-progress" photos and the final product
from the chalk artist on the layout.

"The Magic of Disney Animation"

by Pam Talluto
Rochester Hills, MI
S U P P L I E S

Patterned paper: NRN Designs
Die cuts: Accu-Cut Systems
Circle punches: Family Treasures
Alphabet letters: "Fat Dot," Repositionable
Sticky Die-Cut Letters, Provo Craft
Computer font: CK Toggle, "The Best of Creative
Lettering" CD Vol. 2, *Creating Keepsakes*

Disneyland

The Snyder Family visiting Disneyland; June, 1998.

◄ James, Nichole, Edward, and Michelle Snyder.

Nichole and James on "Alice in Wonderland."

It's a beautiful day to be in the Magic Kingdom. Nichole and James enjoy some shade and beautiful flowers while they take a break to make a plan for the day.

Nichole, Mom, and James taking a spin in the tea cups on the "Mad Tea Party" ride in Fantasyland.

"Disneyland"

by Michelle Snyder
Nampa, ID

S U P P L I E S

Rectangle punch (on filmstrip): Punchline, McGill
Mickey Mouse punch: All Night Media
Pens: My Legacy Writer and Scrapbook Writers,
Close To My Heart/D.O.T.S.
Mickey hat: Michelle's own design
Title: Michelle copied the Disneyland logo
for the layout title.

"New Orleans Square"

by Karan Simoni
Antioch, CA

S U P P L I E S

Red hologram paper: Sandylion
Patterned paper: Paper Pizazz, Hot Off The Press
Scissors: Imperial edge, Fiskars
Pen: Hybrid Gel Roller, Pentel
Computer font: Scrap Family,
Lettering Delights Vol. 1, Inspire Graphics
Idea to note: Karan made the mask using
Zucker Feather Products, gold ribbon,
a gold-lace doily from Amscan and
a rosebud by Offray.

Paper edge: Corkscrew by Fiskars; Die cuts: Pebbles in my Pocket (clipboard); Ellison (hat); Die-cut art by Nancy Church of Augusta, GA

"Candy Castle"

by Lori Bergmann
Turlock, CA
Photos by Dawn Leighter
Centerville, UT

S U P P L I E S

Scissors: Jumbo Scallop edge, Provo Craft;
Scallop edge, Fiskars

Lettering template: Scrapbook, Provo Craft

Circle punches: Family Treasures

Corner slot punch: Double scallop, Family Treasures

Pens: Milky Gel Roller, Pentel

Patterned paper: Lori's own design

Disney World
Itinerary...

1. Wake up early
2. Ride the Monorail
3. Visit Cinderella's Castle
4. Take lots of pictures
5. Ride Space Mountain
6. Get Mickey's Autograph!

Memorabilia Idea

As an alternative to a

photograph, have a cast member

draw your silhouette.

EPCOT
World Showcase

We had a great time visiting all eleven countries in the World Showcase. We got a passport at the beginning and had it stamped and signed at each country we visited. It was fun sampling native foods, seeing famous landmarks and talking to people that were really from that particular country.

United Kingdom

Canada

"Epcot World Showcase"

by Pam Talluto
Rochester Hills, MI

SUPPLIES

Lettering template: Block, ABC Tracers, EK Success

Patterned paper (navy with white speckles): Families are Forever

Punches: Family Treasures

Computer font: CK Toggle, "The Best of Creative Lettering" CD Vol. 2, *Creating Keepsakes*

World: Pam's own design

Memorabilia idea: Pam included an Epcot Passport on the layout.

EPCOT CENTER

Jason and I got free tickets to the Epcot Center. We took these pictures while we waited for the park to open. We finished our day off watching the light show and fireworks. They were spectacular!

What a stud!

August 1997 Orlando, Florida

"Epcot Center"

by Nancy Church
Augusta, GA

SUPPLIES

Patterned paper: Provo Craft
Stationery (flags): Bo-Bunny Press
Lettering template: Block, ABC Tracers, EK Success
Computer font: Doodle Basic, PagePrintables, Cock-A-Doodle Design Inc.

"Keeping Cool at Epcot"

by Ellen James
Orem, UT

SUPPLIES

Stickers: Design Lines, Mrs. Grossman's
Sandals and lemonade accents: PagePieces, Cock-A-Doodle Design Inc.

Kid stickers: me & my BIG ideas
Lettering idea: CK Expedition, "The Best of Creative Lettering" CD Vol. 1, *Creating Keepsakes*
Pen: Zig Writer, EK Success
Colored pencils: Memory Pencils, EK Success

Keeping COOL at Epcot

"Tower of Terror™"

by Tara Whittle

Troy, NY

SUPPLIES

Pen: Zig Memory System, EK Success

Lettering idea: Tara's own design (adapted from the ride logo)

Memorabilia idea: Tara included a Hollywood Tower Hotel tag from
the ride and a ride photo in its souvenir photo folder on the layout.

Paper edge: Corkscrew by Fiskars

"Walk Around the World"
by Liisa Froggatt
Valencia, CA
SUPPLIES
Hexagon template: Memories Forever, Westrim
Pens: Le Plume II, Marvy Uchida
Chalk: Craf-T Products

"Typhoon Lagoon™"
by Michael Delacruz
San Diego, CA
SUPPLIES
Patterned paper (clouds): Frances Meyer
Ship paper piecing: Michael's own design
Pirate flag sticker: Stickopotamus
Circle punches: Family Treasures

Stickers: Stickopotamus (fishing theme stickers); Frances Meyer (splashes and wood); PrintWorks (vines)
Pens: Zig Writers, EK Success
Memorabilia idea: Michael included a Typhoon Lagoon brochure on the layout.

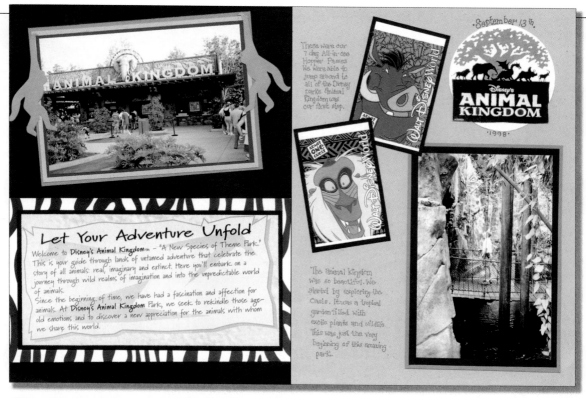

"Let Your Adventure Unfold"

by Victoria Kortt
Lethbridge, AB, Canada

SUPPLIES

Patterned paper: Frances Meyer
Monkey die cuts: Accu-Cut Systems
Animal Kingdom logo: Victoria copied and
enlarged the logo from a Walt Disney
World information booklet.

Idea to note: Victoria copied and
enlarged a section of a Disney's
Animal Kingdom brochure and used
it as a title and as journaling on
the left side of the layout.

Memorabilia idea: Victoria included her
Disney park passes on the layout.

"Disney's Animal Kingdom"

by Carrie Barton
Pendleton, IN

SUPPLIES

Die cuts: ScrapEase, What's New Ltd.
Pens: Zig Writer, EK Success; Le Plume II, Marvy Uchida
Souvenir photo, frame and logo: Walt Disney World

"Disney's Animal Kingdom Safari Adventure"

by Victoria Kortt
Lethbridge, AB, Canada
SUPPLIES

Giraffe sticker: Sandylion
Pen: Zig Writer, EK Success
Jeep and sign: Victoria's own design
Idea to note: Victoria used Funky Fur by Grafix for the spare tire on the back of the jeep.

"Diggin' Dinos"

by Gwen M. Aberle
Harwood, ND
SUPPLIES

Background paper: Provo Craft
Velveteen and Diamond Dust paper: Paper Adventures
Computer fonts: CK Journaling, "The Best of Creative Lettering" CD Vol. 2, *Creating Keepsakes*
Pen: Zig Millennium, EK Success
Chalk: Craf-T Products
Mickey, Pluto and dinosaur paper piecing: Idea from a Disney coloring book
Bone lettering idea: Gwen's own design

Paper edge: Corkscrew by Fiskars

"Cruise'n"

by Megan McMurdie
Rochester Hills, MI
Photos by Kim Sand
Spanish Fork, UT
SUPPLIES
Pens: Zig Writers, EK Success; Milky Gel Roller, Pentel
Banner: Megan's own design

"Disney Magic"

by Becki Engler
Hercules, CA
SUPPLIES
Patterned paper: The Paper Patch
Vellum: The Paper Company
Border stickers: Mrs. Grossman's

Paper edge: Corkscrew by Fiskars; Die cut: Ellison; Die-cut art by Nancy Church of Augusta, GA

"Disney Cruise"
by Marla Bird
Pebbles in my Pocket
Orem, UT
SUPPLIES
Computer fonts: CK Anything Goes,
"The Best of Creative Lettering" CD Vol. 1
and CK Toggle, "The Best of Creative Lettering"
CD Vol. 2, *Creating Keepsakes*
Die cut: Ellison
Colored pencils: Prismacolor, Sanford
Memorabilia idea: Marla included a Guest of
Honor button from the cruise on the layout.

"DCL Magic"
by Ruth Ann Geer-Lloyd
Enola, PA
SUPPLIES
Mickey punches: All Night Media
Alphabet letters: "Scrapbook"
Alphabitties, Repositionable Sticky
Die-Cut Letters, Provo Craft
Computer font: Nite Club,
downloaded from the Internet
Life preserver template: Nautical,
Theme Stencils, Pebbles in my Pocket
Pen: Zig Writer, EK Success
Title: Ruth copied the Disney Cruise
Line logo from a brochure
Memorabilia idea: Ruth included a Disney
Cruise itinerary on the layout.

"Castaway Cay"

by Ruth Ann Geer-Lloyd
Enola, PA
SUPPLIES
Computer font (title): Misfit, downloaded from the Internet
Mickey punches: All Night Media
Corner slot punch: Double Scallop, Family Treasures
Scissors: Deckle edge, Fiskars
Starfish die cuts: Stamping Station

Psychedelic embossing powder: Stamp Express
Computer font (journaling): CK Script, "The Best of Creative Lettering" CD Vol. 1, *Creating Keepsakes*
Pen: Zig Writer, EK Success
Palm tree: Ruth Ann's own design
Memorabilia idea: Ruth Ann included an itinerary and stamps on the layout.

"Sand-Castle Building 101"

by Holly Clark
Temple, TX
SUPPLIES
Die cuts: Ellison
Scissors: Deckle edge, Fiskars
Footprint punch: Marvy Uchida
Computer font: Disney Print, QuarkXPress
Castles, flags and sand: Holly's own designs

Postcard sent from the post office on Castaway Cay

Paper edge: Corkscrew by Fiskars

"Castaway Cay Bahamas"
by Becki Engler
Hercules, CA
S U P P L I E S
Patterned paper: The Paper Company
Computer font: DJ Jenn Pen, Fontastic! Vol. 2, D.J. Inkers
Memorabilia idea: Becki included a Disney postcard on the layout.

we woke up the second morning docked at Castaway Cay, Disney's private island, where we spent the entire day sunning, snorkeling, playing and swimming. The day on Castaway Cay was Travis' favorite part of the trip!

"Castaway Cay"
by Megan McMurdie
Rochester Hills, MI
Photos by Kim Sand
Spanish Fork, UT
S U P P L I E S
Pens: Zig Writer and Zig Millennium, EK Success
Palm tree and umbrella: Megan's own designs

As we pulled up to the white sand beaches, we definitely felt like we were on our own private island. Our days were filled with entertainment!

eces to the Puzzle!

Paperkins™

Making paper dolls has never been easier... just assemble and glue together! Every package comes complete with all the cardstock-cut pieces for making one Paperkins™ Paper Doll (plus lots of extras for page scenes). 48 Collectable styles available.

Circle Scissor™

As simple as drawing a circle... now you can cut up to 125 different circles! A companion to Circle Ruler,™ this *Pen Blade* and ball-bearing *Rotating Disc* makes a clean one-motion circle cut. Available with or without "Cutting Mat". Extra *Pen Blades* and *Spare Blades* sold separately.

Patent Pending

Paper Shapers™

Now there's a better way to punch your paper into shape! The patented Paper Shapers™ "thumb punch™" makes a neat and clean punch while being gentle on your hands. 24 Basic Shaper designs - in *cool* clear colors!

ABC Tracers™

Alphabet templates that make anyone an expert in creative lettering! Six different alphabet styles made of heavyweight see-through plastic are perfect for coloring, detailing or cutting out. 1¼" size letters: Block Upper, Block Lower, Dot Upper, Dot Lower plus Funky and Log Cabin. "Tracer Tips" book also available.

Border Buddy®

The ultimate bordering template for creative scrapbooking! Every versatile design includes tons of bordering patterns and corners for making exceptional pages. 12 designs available in both Original and Junior sizes - plus "Borders and Beyond" idea books, too!

Patent Pending

EK
SUCCESS

Clifton, NJ
w.eksuccess.com

by Kristy Banks

Try These Easy Borders!
Featuring Mickey Mouse and Winnie the Pooh

Make some magic with these 11 borders

I F YOU'RE STUMPED FOR THE PERFECT border to enhance your layout, look no further. Here are 11 ideas that will frame your pages with the colorful flair that they deserve.

MICKEY MOUSE

No trip to a Disney resort would be complete without meeting Mickey Mouse. So check out these border ideas that'll be worthy of those fun photos (see Figure 1). If you're short on time, consider All Night Media's Mickey profile punch, which adds an instant touch of Disney. Used in conjunction with travel stickers, it creates a striking border for your travel photos. Or, use it to highlight your millennial visit to "the Happiest Place on Earth." All Night Media also offers a Mickey silhouette punch—just add a polka dot bow, and it's a Minnie Mouse silhouette.

If these punches aren't in your stash, pull out your circle and hole punches (see Figure 2). The sihouette of Mickey Mouse is a snap—simply punch a large circle and adhere two smaller ones to it. If you're making a Mousketeer™ layout, just trim the larger circle, and you've created your own mouseketeer hat for your happy troops.

If your little one celebrated a Disney-themed birthday, check out the festive border in Figure 3. I used colored vellum and a balloon and circle punch to make the Mickey Mouse balloons. I made the "Mylar" balloons from metallic paper, then adhered stickers to the paper. Finally, I used very thin strips of paper to make the curly balloon strings.

WINNIE THE POOH

You've probably noticed that Winnie the Pooh is a favorite among kids of all ages. So for photos of your favorite bear, why not try one of these fun borders (see Figure 4). In the first, I tore brown paper to make the "dirt," used the birch-leaf punch to make the green foliage, then placed the stickers along the border. In the second, I used a square punch, then placed the figures over the squares. Finally, I added festive mini-flower and balloon punches.

MICKEY'S FRIENDS

Your pages wouldn't be complete without Mickey's friends. For your photos of those legendary pals, try the easy border options in Figure 5. *Note:* In the first, I silhouetted the stickers and placed them inside the

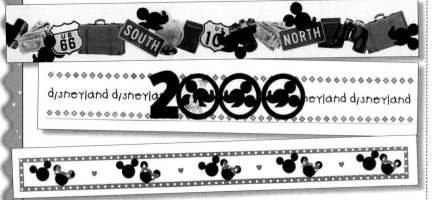

Figure 1. A punch featuring a Mickey Mouse silhouette adds an instant touch of Disney to any border. *Borders by Kristy Banks of Highland, UT.* **"Travel" Supplies** *Stickers:* Frances Meyer; *Mickey punch:* All Night Media. **"2000"** *Diamond rub-on transfer:* Provo Craft; *Computer font:* DJ Crayon, Fontastic!, D.J. Inkers; *Stickers:* Source unknown; *Mickey punch:* All Night Media. **"True Love"** *Mickey punch:* All Night Media; *Triangle punch:* McGill; *Heart punch:* Fiskars; *Patterned paper:* Frame-Ups Paper Coordinates, My Mind's Eye.

frames of the filmstrip. In the second, scrapbooker Nancy Church cut the characters from a piece of Hot Off The Press Disney paper, then adhered them to gold-colored paper.

If you have photos of other characters but can't find a sticker or punch that represents them, simply incorporate elements from their costumes (or movies they're associated with) to make your borders. The rope, sheriff stars and color and pattern schemes in Figure 6 are readily associated with Woody from *Toy Story*.

There you have it—11 samples that will help you create magical borders for your layouts. ♥

Figure 2. Use two circle-punch sizes to make your own Mickey borders. *Borders by Kim McCrary of Pleasant Grove, UT ("Disneyland 2000"); Kristy Banks of Highland, UT ("Mouseketeers").* **"Disneyland 2000" Supplies** *Circle punches:* Family Treasures; *Computer font:* CK Toggle, "The Best of Creative Lettering" CD Vol. 2, *Creating Keepsakes; Stickers:* Frances Meyer. **"Mouseketeers"** *Square stickers:* Alphabet Blocks, S.R.M. Press Inc.; *Punches:* Family Treasures (circle, flower, cloud, star); Marvy Uchida (sun); All Night Media (border); *"Smile face" rubber stamp:* Stampendous.

Figure 3. Celebrate your Disney memories with this festive border. *Border by Kristy Banks of Highland, UT.* **Supplies** *Balloon punch:* McGill; *Circle punch:* Family Treasures; *Mickey and Minnie stickers:* Sandylion; *Pen:* Zig Opaque Writer, EK Success; *Star stickers:* Mrs. Grossman's.

Figure 4. These borders featuring Winnie the Pooh are sweet as "hunny." *Borders by Kristy Banks of Highland, UT.* **"In the Garden" Supplies** *Leaf punch:* Family Treasures; *Winnie the Pooh stickers:* Sandylion. **"Celebration"** *Punches:* All Night Media (Pooh, Tiger, square, balloon); Family Treasures (flower).

Figure 5. These border ideas will help you spotlight Mickey's friends. *Borders by Kristy Banks of Highland, UT ("Filmstrip"); Nancy Church of Augusta, GA ("Mickey and friends").* **"Filmstrip" Supplies** *Stickers:* Sandylion; *Border punch:* Family Treasures; **"Cast of Characters"** *Disney characters:* Hot Off The Press; *Polka dot paper:* The Paper Patch.

Figure 6. Take elements from a character's costume or movie to make a customized border. *Border by Kristy Banks of Highland, UT.* **Supplies** *Cloud and star punches:* Family Treasures; *Hole punch:* Punchline, McGill; *Rope rub-on transfer:* Provo Craft; *Pens:* Zig Writer and Zig Scroll & Brush, EK Success.

Power Punch for All Your Punch-Art Needs

Whether you're making a polka-dot border for your pictures with Minnie Mouse or a jungle-theme mat for your photos of Jungle Cruise™, punches can add just the right touch. Since you select the paper color, you can ensure that your enhancements complement your layouts.

The Personal Power Punch and the Professional Power Punch by Tapestry in Time will satisfy all your punch-art needs. These lightweight tools are like having a "mini die-cut machine" and will help ensure accurate, nearly effortless punching.

If you're looking for some fun punch-art inspirations, check out our *Bring Your Punches to Life* idea book, which is filled with step-by-step instructions and full-color diagrams.

TAPESTRY IN TIME

Phone: 925/449-3205

Fax: 925/449-3209

Web site: . . . . *www.tapestryintime.com*

MSRP:

Professional Power Punch $79.99

Personal Power Punch $59.99

Bring Your Punches to Life idea book $11.99

so "Minnie" hats!

Eva's first trip to Walt Disney World was perfect. She especially loved trying on the colorful hats. We all agree that the Minnie hat suits her just perfectly!
~ October 1999

Let KODAK *Help You Preserve Your Memories*

Can you recall the wonder in your child's eyes the first time he or she met Mickey Mouse? You'll want to keep your memories as vivid in the future as they are today. And pictures are a great way to keep the memory alive.

Life is full of those special moments, so don't get caught without a way to capture them. Whether you're off to see Mickey Mouse again, or just have a day at the beach planned, be sure to carry a KODAK MAX flash one-time-use camera with you—it provides a quick, easy way to take pictures any-

time, anywhere. The camera is pre-loaded with 39 exposures of KODAK MAX film. Take it to a local store that offers KODAK Picture Processing to get it developed, and you'll get your pictures back on new Duralife paper, so you can be assured they will last for generations.

Once you get your pictures back, it's time to start scrapbooking! Highlight those extra-special shots by using the KODAK Picture Maker to enlarge a photo or zoom in on the most important elements. You can even add text and borders to a photo, or turn a color

photo into a black-and-white one, with the Picture Maker.

Remember, nothing captures life's special moments better than pictures—and nothing tells stories better than a scrapbook. Let Kodak help you tell your story!

KODAK
Phone: 800/242-2424
Web site: . . . . *www.kodak.com*

Great Storage Ideas

Don't let your memories be forgotten—get them easily into your beautiful Generations™ by Hazel® Album using a wide array of incredible Generations by Hazel products.

Scrapbooking your photos will be a snap with Generations' Crop Station™ Rolling Organizer—the ultimate workstation on wheels. The main compartment is large enough to hold a 12" x 15" album and contains a removable paper/pen organizer for protecting and storing pages that are "in progress." The Crop Station's mesh and clear pockets keep contents in plain view. Inside the station are plenty of loops, so you can organize your scissors, pens, punches and cutters—providing scrapbook supplies at your fingertips while your work space is free from clutter.

Safely display memorabilia from your trip in the 12" x 12" Memorabilia Pockets™, which are made with translucent archival polypropylene. The pockets can also be used to store die cuts, stickers and "in-progress" layouts.

If you're in need of additional organizational tools, check out the Memory Express™ and Photo Express™ storage units. The expandable compartments are ideal for carrying and organizing paper, scissors and photographs as

well as sticker sheets and die cuts.

Safely store your 3" x 5" and 4" x 6" photos (as well as VHS tapes) in Generations' durable archival, acid free and water-resistant Poly Photo Box.

GENERATIONS BY HAZEL

Phone: 800/262-7261

Web site: . . . . *www.generationsbyhazel.com*

MSRP:

12" x 12" Tapestry Album	$35.99
Crop Station Rolling Organizer	$129.99
Memory Express	$17.99
Photo Express.	$11.99
Memorabilia Pockets (package of 3)	$4.99
Poly Photo Box	$7.99

Layout by: Brenda Bennett; Photos on layout by: Doug Larson; Disney characters © Disney Enterprises, Inc.

Layout by: Cock-A-Doodle Design, Inc.; Disney characters © Disney Enterprises, Inc.

Lacey, Maddie, Mickey and Kennedy
One of our favorite parts of Disneyland was meeting Mickey and Minnie and visiting them in their own house. Mickey gave us all a big wet kiss on the cheek!
Disneyland 1999

Let Cock-A-Doodle Design Show You the Secret to Making Perfect Pages

PAGETOPPERS™

Instantly add a fun title to your layout with Cock-A-Doodle Design's PageToppers™. You're sure to find one that expresses your theme among their more than 100 popular page headings.

MSRP: $0.35

PAGEDOODLERS™

These waterproof, fade-proof permanent markers are sure to add a splash to any layout. Their even-flow tips produce vibrant, consistent colors. Available in packages of 12 or sold singly, these markers are sure to please even the most discriminating scrapbooker.

MSRP: . . . . $3.00 each

PAGEPRINTABLES™

In search of a distinctive computer font to add journaling to your layout? Well look no further—choose from 15 True Type fonts on the PagePrintables™ CD. Also be sure to check out the 64 new PageToppers™ (which are exclusive to this CD) as well as 10 colorized alphabets.

MSRP: $19.95

PAGEFRAMES™

Cock-A-Doodle Design's PageFrames™ will help you frame your photos with ease. These acid- and lignin-free cardstock frames work with your 3" x 5" and 4" x 6" photos and add instant charm to your layout.

MSRP: . . . . $0.40–$0.60

PAGEPIECES™

Looking for an enhancement to tie your layout together gracefully? PagePieces are illustrated die cuts that complement our PageToppers™ and PageFrames™. The PagePieces™ are sold in strips that contain two to three different images.

MSRP: . . . . $0.50 per strip

We give you something to crow about!

COCK-A-DOODLE DESIGN, INC.

E-mail: . . . . *info@cockadoodledesign.com*

Web site: . . . . *www.cockadoodledesign.com*

Phone: . . . . 800/262-9727 or 801/954-0554

Memorabilia Pockets

The 3L Memorabilia Pockets are perfect for storing:

- Monorail driver's licenses
- Parking passes
- Membership passports
- Souvenir coins and tokens
- Photo CDs
- 8 mm/VHS-C videocassettes
- . . . and more!

Taylor fell in love with Minnie. When Taylor saw Minnie, she ran up to her and gave her a big hug. Taylor sat on Minnie's lap for a few minutes and told her that she was having so much fun in Minnie's house. Then we snapped this photo of our sweet little girl and her new best friend.

Having trouble saving and storing important memorabilia from your Disney vacation? 3L Memorabilia Pockets are the perfect solution! These archival-safe pockets have a removable-adhesive flap to keep important memories safe and secure while allowing you to take the keepsake out and replace it over and over again.

Don't forget to mount your other memories with 3L PhotoFix. Each self-adhesive mounting square is archival safe and lignin free to make sure your photos and other mounted items stay secure on your pages. Or, use 3L Archival-safe Photo Corners, the ultimate in photo conservation. They add a special elegance and decoration to any photo—from the *Main Street Electrical Parade* to that special photo with Mickey Mouse. And they're self-adhesive, so you don't have to lick 'em to stick 'em!

3L CORP.

Phone:	800/828-3130
Web site:	*www.3LCorp.com*
E-mail:	*mail@3LCorp.com*

MSRP:

Memorabilia Pockets	$2.99
PhotoFix	$3.49
Archival-safe Photo Corners	$3.99-4.99

Personalize Your Scrapbook Albums

Nothing's quite as personal as your scrapbook. It tells the stories of a lifetime and contains the photos of those dear to you. So when the time comes to put your precious memories into an album, make sure the cover is as unique as the contents!

Let GoldStamp Creations goldstamp the covers and spines of your Westrim, Webway and Creative Memories cloth or leather strap-hinge albums. Choose from over 400 popular titles, or create your own. With a customized cover and spine, you can easily find your "Disney Vacation" or "Our Wedding" album among all the others on the shelf.

Sometimes you really can tell a book by its cover, and GoldStamp Creations will help yours reflect both your pride and your creativity—satisfaction guaranteed!

GOLDSTAMP CREATIONS

Phone: . . . . Toll-free 877/456-4561

Web site: . . . . www.GOLDSTAMP.com

E-mail: . . . . service@goldstamp.com

MSRP:

Front cover . . . . $8.00 as shown

Complete spine . . . . $12.00 as shown

GoldStamp Creations™

Double-Ended Markers

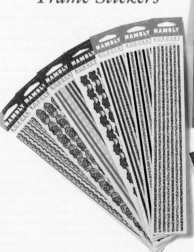

Available in white, black, blue, red, green, yellow, violet and orange.

ZEBRA®

Also available from Zebra Pen, Jimnie® Gel Rollerballs in assorted colors: antique, traditional and metallic.

Whether you're writing a title on your layout or drawing a border, Zebra's Craft-Star™ double-ended markers are sure to add that extra touch of magic.

The Craft-Star™ markers are easy to use. While the cap is on, shake the pen well. Remove the cap, and press the pen's tip on a sheet of paper until the ink appears. Then you're ready to write.

The ink colors can be layered without bleeding together. Simply draw one color and let it dry before applying another one. For a softer, more blended effect, layer the second color before the first is fully dry. Use the white marker to create pastels.

For additional flexibility, the marker is double ended. The 2 mm bullet-point end of the marker is ideal for journaling, creating your own borders or tracing around stencils. The 8 mm chisel-tip end works well for bold lettering styles that require heavy ink coverage.

The Craft-Star™ double-ended marker is ideal for use on all types of paper, poster board, wood, polymer clay, metal, glass, fabric and more. Available in eight brilliant colors, these pens are sure to add verve to your layouts.

ZEBRA PEN CORP.

Phone: 800/247-7170
Web site: . . . . *www.zebrapen.com*
E-mail: . . . . *zebrainfo@zebrapen.com*
MSRP: $4.98

Layout by: Brenda Bennett; Photos by: Doug Larson; Disney characters © Disney Enterprises, Inc.

Border, Corner and Frame Stickers

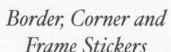

HAMBLY STUDIOS

If you're looking for a quick and simple way to enhance your photos, check out Hambly Studios' new border, corner and frame stickers. We've made scrapbooking even easier with our new Scrapbook Stuff kits, which contain die cuts, stickers, photo frames and paper—everything you need!

Available in themes to match just about any photo, these stickers make a terrific addition to any layout.

HAMBLY STUDIOS INC.

Phone: . 800/451-3999 (wholesale only)
E-mail: . *hamblystudios@worldnet.att.net*
MSRP:

Stickers: . . . . $1.25–$2.00
Scrapbook Stuff kits . . . . . $3.00–$6.00

Layout by: Brenda Bennett; Photos by: Laurie Green

If you're like most scrap- bookers, you're probably hunting for a tool that'll make your hobby easier, quicker and more fun. For cutting photo mats, journaling blocks and other straight edges, there's no question about it— CARL's rotary paper trimmers are the best. The trimmers cut more pre- cisely, more smoothly and more safely than any other rotary trimmer in the world.

If you're looking for a decorative edge to add a little snap to your lay- outs, CARL has recently introduced a dozen interchangeable decorative- edge cutting disks, which can be used with most CARL Rotary Trimmers. Available in the most popu- lar edges (Deckle, Victorian, Colonial and Zig Zag, just to name a few), these new blades are an affordable way to add a precise yet creative flair to your layouts.

CARL MFG. USA INC.

Phone: 847/956-0730

E-mail: . . . CARL@CARL-Products.com

Address:

CARL Manufacturing USA Inc.

1862 South Elmhurst Road

Prospect, IL 60056

MSRP: . . . .

Rotary Trimmers . . . $13.99–$600.00

Decorative-edge blades . $5.99–$6.99

CARL.®

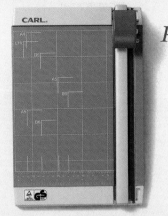

Rotary Paper Trimmer

---

by A l y s s a   A l l g a i e r

Memorable Memorabilia

While visiting Disney theme parks, don't forget to collect memorabilia. You don't have to scrapbook everything, but it's nice to have lots of appealing options. Keep these memorabilia suggestions in mind:

- Trip itinerary
- Travel agency brochures
- Airline tickets
- Receipts (from restaurants, shops, hotel, rental car)
- Park passes
- Maps (park and road)
- Guides
- Programs
- Brochures
- Tour schedules

- Parking passes
- Characters' autographs
- Smashed pennies (made in machines all over the parks)
- Postcards
- Stationery from hotel
- Napkins
- Swizzle sticks
- Empty candy bags
- Smashed-down popcorn boxes

- Other found items (If the item is too big to fit in your scrapbook, take a picture of a family member holding the item. Pair it with some lively explanatory journaling.) ♥

"The Happiest" Place on Earth™"
by Becky Higgins
Peoria, AZ
Photos by Laurie Green
Alpine, UT
S U P P L I E S
Circle punches (Mickey silhouette): McGill
Pen: Zig Writer, EK Success
Idea to note: Becky used Archival Mist to de- acidify the memorabilia.

125 *Tantalizing Titles to Enliven Your Layouts*

Catchy titles can contribute so much to your scrapbook layouts! They can grab the eye, set the tone, enhance the impact of your photos and even help you to focus your design theme. There's no more effective or enjoyable way to express your unique personality in your pages than with clever, evocative titles. Set your mind free, and be your funniest, most poetic or most sardonic self! The following suggestions will help you to make your layouts as vibrant and whimsical as your memories!

TITLES FOR POPULAR RIDES OR LOCATIONS

- "A Pirate's Life for Me," "Argh, Matey," "Set Sail for an Adventure," "Anchors Aweigh!" "Loose Cannons," "Our Ship-Shape Sweeties," "Shiver Me Timbers!" "High-Seas Shenanigans," "Pure Piracy," "Makin' Waves," "Walking Planks (and Other Pranks)" . . . . *Pirates of the Caribbean*™

- "A 'Douse' of Fun," "Our Laughin' Place," "Getting Soaked," "A Deluge (with No Rain Cloud in Sight!)," " Making a Splash," "All Wet," "Taking a Dive," "Rinse Cycle," "Watered Down," "Not a Dry Eye in the House," "Showered with Delight" . . . . *Splash Mountain*™

- "The Wildest Ride in the Wilderness," "Hang on to Your Hats," "There's Treasure in Them Thar Hills," "All Aboard!" "Basic 'Train'ing," "On the Right Track," "Express Train to Memoryville," "Kids 'n Cabooses" . . . . *Big Thunder Mountain Railroad*™

- "A Ride in Our 'Doom Buggy'," "Tomb, Sweet Tomb," "Cobwebs and Creaks," "Skeletons in the Closet," "Scaring up Some Fun," "A Screaming Good Time," "Haunted but Undaunted" . . . . *The Haunted Mansion*™

- "A Palace for Our Princess," "The 'Royal' Treatment," "A Castle that 'In-Spires'," "Castle, Sweet Castle," "Crowning Moments," "Fit for a Queen," "The Forecast Calls for 'Reign'," "Where Love Rules," "Having a 'Ball' at the Castle" . . . . *Cinderella Castle*™ or *Sleeping Beauty Castle*™

- "Tea for Two," "Twistin' and Turnin'," "We Had a 'Reel'y Great Time!" "In a Tizzy over Tea," "Sugar, No Lemon," "No Time for Crumpets!" "It Suited Us to a 'Tea'," "Eyes Big as Saucers!" "A Swirling Sea of Tea," "Jolly Good Fun," "A Big Sip of Squeals". . . . . *Mad Tea Party*™

- "Hóla! Güten Tag! Hello!" "The Universal Language". . . . . *It's a Small World*™

- "An Awesome Alcove," "Mermaid Memories," "Undercurrents of Radiance," "Whirlpools of Wonder," "Waves and Caves," "A Lot o' Grotto" . . . . *Ariel's Grotto*™

- "Full Speed Ahead," "Keeping Your Momentum," "High-Speed Cruiser," "No Speed Limit!" "On the Fast Track" . . . . *Test Track*™

- "Going Galactic," "A Shot in the Dark," "Heavens!" "Where's Pluto?" "Outer Space Is Our Kind of Place," "What a Blast!" "A Stellar Adventure," "Many Moons Ago," "Our Space Odyssey," "Moonwalk, Anyone?" . . . . *Space Mountain*™

- "Flying High," "Tusk, Tusk!" "Ears that Steer," "So Flighty!" "High and Mighty Cute" . . . .
. . . . *Dumbo the Flying Elephant*™

- "It's a Jungle Out There," "Cruisin' through Life" . . . . *Jungle Cruise*™

- "Hooked on the Captain," "Deep in the Heart of Never Land," "A 'Darling' Ride" . . . .
. . . . *Peter Pan's Flight*™

TITLES FOR PHOTOS WITH DISNEY CHARACTERS

- "The Better to Hear You With," "A Hug from Mickey," "The Sorcerer (and Some Little Apprentices)" . . . . Mickey Mouse

- "Minnie and Me," "All Ears" . . . . Minnie Mouse

- "Everything's Just Ducky," "Pure Quackery!" "He Fills the Bill," "Ruffled Feathers," . . . .
. . . . Donald Duck

- "Just Goofin' Around," "Spoofy!" . . . . Goofy

- "So 'Bear'y Special," "Bear Hugs," "'Bear'ly Noticeable," "'Bear'ing it Gracefully"
. . . . Winnie the Pooh

- "It's Enchanting to Meet You" . . . . Snow White

- "The Royal Treatment," "Princess Charming," "Our Highness," "Enthroned in Our Hearts," "No Curtsies Required," "Long Live the Princess!" . . . . Meeting one of the princesses

TITLES FOR EATING

- "An Insatiable Appetite"
- "Delicious Diversions"
- "The Magic of Disappearing Food"
- "Feast for the Famished"
- "Hungry for More"
- "Served up with Character"
- "Nosh Niblin'"

GENERIC TITLES FOR DISNEY-THEMED PHOTOS

- "A Cast of Characters"
- "The Three Mouseketeers"
- "Babes in Joyland"
- "Our Royal Family"
- "Always Land"
- "Party Animals"

Paper-piecing art by Brenda Bennett of Morenci, AZ

www.heartlandpaper.com

...the scrapbook store in your home

The Heartland Paper Co.

MAGICAL FAMILY
MEMORIES

"Breanne's just **GOOFIN** around"

"Breanne's Just Goofin' Around"

by Heather Thatcher
Draper, UT
Photos by Dawn Leighter
Centerville, UT
SUPPLIES
Patterned paper: Provo Craft
Lettering idea: CK Groovy,

"The Best of Creative Lettering"
CD Vol. 2, *Creating Keepsakes*
Pens: Zig Writer and Zig Textile,
EK Success
Colored pencils: Prismacolor, Sanford
Goofy ears: Heather's own design

Disneyland
2000

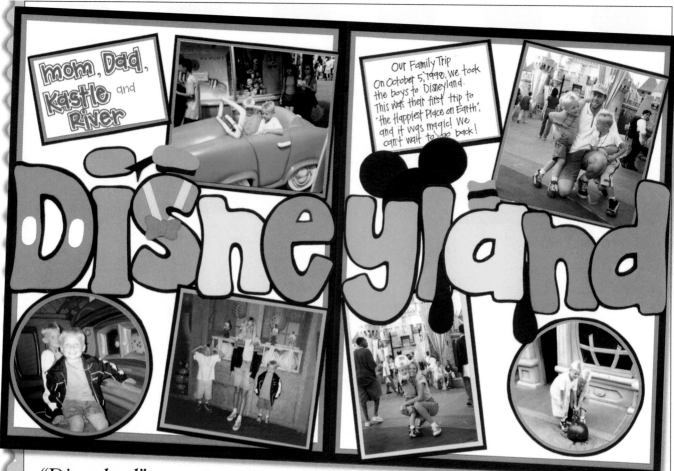

mom, Dad, Kastle and River

Our Family Trip
On October 5, 1998, we took the boys to Disneyland. This was their first trip to "the Happiest Place on Earth", and it was magic! We can't wait to go back!

Disneyland

"Disneyland"
by Jana Francis
Provo, UT
SUPPLIES
Pens: Zig Writers, EK Success
Lettering idea: Jana's own design

"Mickey"
by Bonnie Blumenstock
Pebbles in my Pocket
Orem, UT
SUPPLIES
Patterned paper: The Paper Patch
Mickey Mouse stationery: Paper Pizazz, Hot Off The Press
Lettering template: Block, ABC Tracers, EK Success
Pen: Zig Writer, EK Success

MICKEY

"Disney World 1998"
by Susan E. Marzocchi
New York, NY
S U P P L I E S
Peek-a-Boo Mickey stationery: Paper Pizazz,
Hot Off The Press
Alphabet letters: "Kids" Alphabitties,
Repositionable Sticky Die-Cut Letters,
Provo Craft
Circle punches: Marvy Uchida

"Shake It!"
by Nancy Church
Augusta, GA
Photos by Dawn Leighter
Centerville, UT
S U P P L I E S
Patterned paper: The Paper Patch
Lettering template: Wacky, Frances Meyer
Circle punch: Family Treasures
Computer font: DJ Jumble,
Scraps & Stitches, D.J. Inkers
Tambourine: Nancy's own design

Breanne can find fun out of almost anything! While waiting in line for the Pirates of the Carribean ride, Breanne had a great time playing the tambourine with the drum band. Even the band members were excited by her enthusiasm to join in the fun! She really had her hips a movin'!

Paper edge: Corkscrew by

Disneyland

February 1998
This was our second trip to Disneyland and we again did it during mid-winter break. The weather isn't great that time of year, but it's still a lot better than Washington, and the lines are so short! There was an extra perk this time as my brother Don and his family were able to meet us there so we had someone else to enjoy it with!

"Disneyland"
by Diane Garding
North Bend, WA
SUPPLIES

Alphabet letters: "Fat Dot," Repositionable
Sticky Die-Cut Letters, Provo Craft
Punches: All Night Media (Mickey);
Family Treasures (circles)
Computer font: Scrap Oval, Lettering
Delights Vol. 2, Inspire Graphics

"A Day at Disney"
by Nancy Church
Augusta, GA
SUPPLIES

Patterned paper: The Paper Patch
Photo frame: Frame-Ups, My Mind's Eye
Kids: Friends, My Mind's Eye
Alphabet letters: "Kids" Alphabitties, Repositionable
Sticky Die-Cut Letters, Provo Craft
Computer font: Scrap Casual, Lettering Delights
Vol. 1, Inspire Graphics

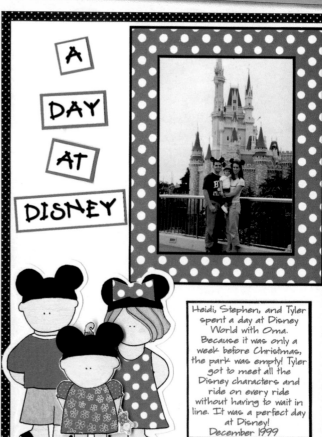

A DAY AT DISNEY

Heidi, Stephen, and Tyler spent a day at Disney World with Oma. Because it was only a week before Christmas, the park was empty! Tyler got to meet all the Disney characters and ride on every ride without having to wait in line. It was a perfect day at Disney!
December 1999

"Doin' the Disney Dance"

by Heather Thatcher
Draper, UT
Photos by Dawn Leighter
Centerville, UT

SUPPLIES

Pens: Zig Writer and Zig Textile, EK Success

Colored pencils: Prismacolor, Sanford

Music bars and notes: Heather's own designs

"Disney"

by Joyce Hill Schweitzer
Greensboro, NC

SUPPLIES

Lettering template: Dream Talk, Close To My Heart/D.O.T.S.

Mickey rubber stamp: Delta Technical Coatings

Ink pad: ColorBox, Clearsnap Inc.

Embossing powder: Mark Enterprises

Pen: Micron Pigma, Sakura

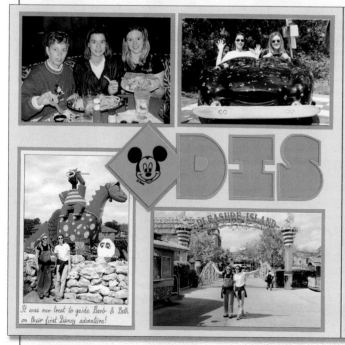

"Disneyland"
by Ellen James
Orem, UT

SUPPLIES

Mickey Mouse and balloon stickers: Sandylion

Pens: Zig Writers, EK Success

Lettering idea: Ellen copied the
Disneyland logo for the layout title.

Memorabilia idea: Ellen included two
Disneyland Flex Signature Passports
on the layout.

"Disneyland"
by Erika Clayton
Pebbles in my Pocket
Orem, UT

SUPPLIES

Patterned paper: The Paper Patch

Alphabet stickers: Pebbles in my Pocket

Mickey Mouse stickers: Sandylion

Pen: Zig Calligraphy, EK Success

Page title: Erika's own design

Memorabilia idea: Erika included her
Disneyland passports on the layout.

Disneyland... the greatest place on Earth!

Best buds share the magic

Theresa, Kari, Nanette, Denise & Debra

celebrate the magic!

Just the Gals!

Do Not Disturb

GUIDEMAP OCT. 11 - 17, 1999

Times & Information

my DISNEY trip

"Disneyland—the Greatest Place on Earth"

by Kari Murphy
Scrappin' Peeps
Olympia, WA

SUPPLIES

Embossed paper: Lasting Impressions for Paper
Patterned paper (blue with white dots): PrintWorks
Photo frames: Frame-Ups, My Mind's Eye
Kids: Friends, My Mind's Eye
Alphabet letters: "Fat Dot," Repositionable
Sticky Die-Cut Letters, Provo Craft
Pen: Zig Writer, EK Success
Memorabilia idea: Kari included a Disneyland
postcard and brochure on the layout.

"My Disney Trip"

by Valerie Dellastatious
Orem, UT

SUPPLIES

Patterned paper: NRN Designs
Page title: PageToppers, Cock-A-Doodle Design Inc.
Memorabilia idea: Don't throw away your
memorabilia—store them in a pocket page.

Memorabilia Idea

Dozens of collectible pins are available during the Millennium Celebration at Walt Disney World.
If you collect any, you may want to include some in your scrapbook.

Paper edge: Corkscrew by Fiskars

Disney Magic

Our family has enjoyed the Magic of Disneyland many times over the years. During our visit in 1998, my mother commented on how much the park had changed over the years and mentioned that she and her parents visited Disneyland the year that it opened. These pictures could be from that visit.

Waiting in line

Betty Spatafore?

Storybook Land Canal Boats

Bob and Betty Spatafore

Storybook Land Canal Boats

Then...

And Now...

Dumbo

Sian, Spenser & Mawrgyn

Betty and Bob Spatafore's grandchild and great-grandchildren

Matt, Mawrgyn, Spenser & Sian

Spatafore, 5 Gen.

Betty and Bob Spatafore's grandchild and great-grandchild

Stacei, Solie & Mario Santana

Alice in Wonderland

Mawrgyn, Solie, Mario & Spenser

These pictures are from our family trip to Disneyland in 1998. On that trip were four generations: Bob, Betty and Brenda Spatafore, Sian and Mawrgyn Roper, Matthew and Spenser Grimm, Stacei, Mario & Solie Santana, Beverly, Joshlyn and Steven Martin.

"Disney Magic, Then and Now"
by Sian L. Roper
Shakopee, MN

SUPPLIES
Lettering and Mickey Mouse: Disney Magic Artist,
Disney Print Studio
Castle: Sian's own design
Computer font: Disney Print, QuarkXPress
Pens: Scrapbook Writer, Close To My Heart/D.O.T.S.

ZIP A DEE DOO DAH

In June, we drove to Disneyland for Nik and Amy to perform with the singing group "Up with Kids". They performed at the Carnation Terrace and both of them sang solos.

June 1999

"Zip-a-dee-doo-dah"

by Shannon Wolz
Salt Lake City, UT
Photos by Jeanne English
Salt Lake City, UT
SUPPLIES
Letter die cuts: The Paper Attic
Paper dolls template: Paper Chain Boy, Provo Craft
Punches: All Night Media (mini spiral); Family Treasures (flower corner rounder, border swirl)
Pens: Gelly Rolls, Sakura; Zig Writer, EK Success
Computer font: CK Print, "The Best of Creative Lettering" CD Vol. 1, *Creating Keepsakes*
Colored pencils: Memory Pencils, EK Success
Doll clothes: Shannon's own designs

"On the Steps of Minnie's House"

by Brenée Williams
Boise, ID
Photos by Peggy Peterson
Park City, UT
SUPPLIES
Patterned paper: Close To My Heart/D.O.T.S.
Scissors: Scallop edge, Fiskars
Circle punch: CARL Mfg.
Hole punch: Punchline, McGill
Pen: Gelly Roll, Sakura
Bow: Brenée's own design

Paper-piecing art by Brenée Williams of Boise, ID

"Our Top 10 List"
by Valerie Strevell
Overland Park, KS
SUPPLIES
Patterned paper: Making Memories
Computer font: DJ FiddleSticks,
FiddleSticks, D.J. Inkers
Clip art: Mickey and Friends Print Studio,
Walt Disney Company

Our Top 10 List!

1. The 50's Prime Time Cafe
2. Kilimanjaro Safaris
3. The Twilight Zone Tower of Terror
4. Honey, I Shrunk The Audience
5. Buzz Lightyear's Space Ranger Spin
6. Big Thunder Mountain Railroad
7. The Barnstormer at Goofy's Wiseacre Farm
8. MuppetVision 3-D
9. Swimming at our hotel in Stormalong Bay
10. Tasting the different sodas from around
    the World at Ice Station Cool

Until Next Time.....

"Disney"
by Jan Tatomir
Farmington Hills, MI
S U P P L I E S
Letter templates: Puzzle Mates

*"Remember the
Magic of Disney"*
by Rachel Lewis
Jacksonville, FL
S U P P L I E S
Mickey and Minnie accents:
Punch-Outs, Hot Off The Press
Mickey punch: All Night Media
Computer font: CK Print, "The Best of
Creative Lettering" CD Vol. 1, *Creating Keepsakes*
Pen: Zig Millennium, EK Success
Lettering idea: From EK Success
Layout idea: Rachel included photos from
two Disney trips to show the passage of
time for both the park and the people.

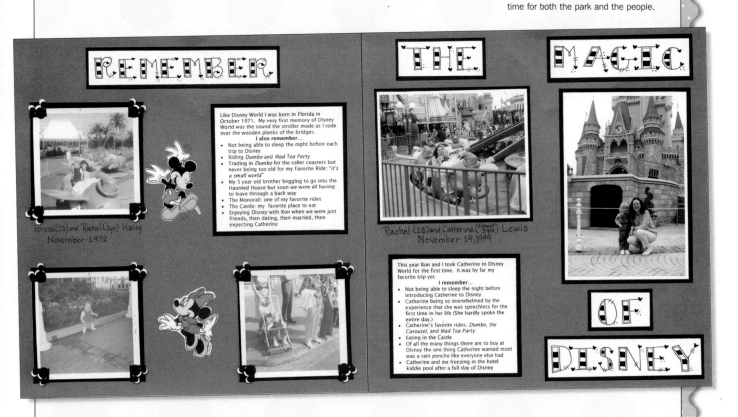

Handwritten text on layout:
- *From DeLynne's home town*
- *Walt Disney Rail Road*
- *Chris & DeLynne*
- *Chris & DeLynne at Cinderella's Castle*
- DEXTER HIGH SCHOOL MARCHING BAND

"Disneyland Memories"

by DeLynne Lahtinen
Seattle, WA

SUPPLIES

Pens: Milky Gel Rollers, Pentel
Mickey pattern: DeLynne got the
idea from a Disney catalog.

Handwritten text on layout:
- Disneyland
- *When you wish upon a star... Your Dreams come true!*

"When You Wish Upon a Star"

by Jana Francis
Provo, UT

SUPPLIES

Patterned paper: NRN Designs
Pens: Zig Writers, EK Success
Castle and clouds: Jana's own designs

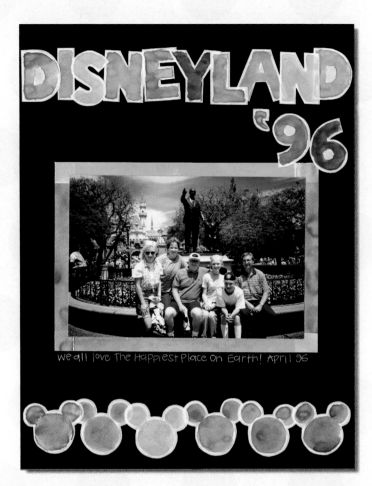

we all love The Happiest Place On Earth! April 96

"Disneyland '96"
Shelly Patten
Pebbles in my Pocket
Orem, UT
SUPPLIES
Lettering template: Block, ABC Tracers, EK Success
Vellum: The Paper Company
Pen: Milky Gel Roller, Pentel
Idea to note: Shelly embossed her title and accents on vellum and then watercolored them.

"Club Disney"
by Lanae Beth Johnson
Glendale, AZ
SUPPLIES
Lettering template: Wacky Letters, Frances Meyer
Wavy ruler: Family Treasures
Balloon die cut: Accu-Cut Systems
Pens: Micron Pigma, Sakura; White Writer Rolling Ball Pen, Sailor

"Catchin' the Disney Bug"

by Heather Thatcher
Draper, UT
SUPPLIES

Patterned paper: Provo Craft
Pens: Zig Writer and Zig Millennium, EK Success;
Gelly Roll, Sakura
Colored pencils: Prismacolor, Sanford
Chalk (on leaves): Craf-T Products
Leaves, grass and ants: Heather's own designs
Idea to note: Flik character was cut from a piece of
wrapping paper.

"Who Wants to Go to Disneyland?"

by Kerri Bradford
Orem, UT
SUPPLIES

Patterned paper: Robin's Nest (yellow striped
and flowered); Scrap Pads, Provo Craft (green)
Vellum: CTI Paper USA Inc.
Lettering template: Block, ABC Tracers, EK Success
Pens: Zig Writer, EK Success; Milky Gel Roller, Pentel
Colored pencils: Prismacolor, Sanford
Punches: Marvy Uchida (star); Family Treasures (daisy)
Computer font: DJ Chunky, Inspirations, D.J. Inkers
Tinkerbell: Idea from the *Peter Pan* video jacket.

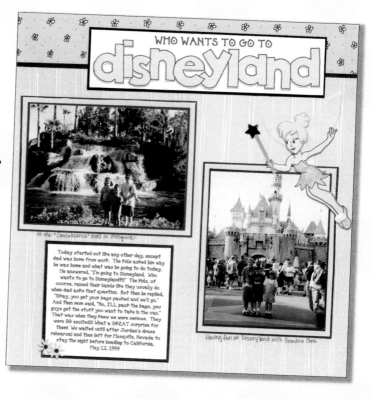

"Ingredients for Disneyland"

by Debi Adams
Anaheim, CA

SUPPLIES

Patterned paper: Close To My Heart/D.O.T.S.

Die cuts: Ellison (filmstrip); Stamping Station (camera); Dayco (Mickey's hands)

Punches: Family Treasures (daisy); All Night Media (Mickey)

Photo frame rubber stamp: D.O.T.S.

Pens: Zig Writers, EK Success

Computer font: Times New Roman, Microsoft Word

Page title: Debi's own design

Vacation Tip

If you are a Three- or Five-Day Flex Passport holder, you may be able to enter the park early. Just inquire about the early-entry days.

"The Happiest Place on Earth"

by Desirée Tanner
Provo Craft
Provo, UT

SUPPLIES

Paper dolls: Coluzzle Paper Doll template, Provo Craft

Roller coaster: Coluzzle Nested Rectangle, Nested Oval and Nested Circle templates, Provo Craft

Scissors: Ripple edge, Fiskars

Flower punch: McGill

Pens: Zig Writer, EK Success; Milky Gel Roller, Pentel

Paper edge: Corkscrew by Fiskars

"Remember the Magic of Disney"
by Tammy Thomas
Oak City, UT
SUPPLIES

Photo frames: Frame-Ups, My Mind's Eye
Computer font: Inn Keeper, source unknown; CK Journaling,
"The Best of Creative Lettering" CD Vol. 2, *Creating Keepsakes*
Pen: Zig Writer, EK Success
Mickey accents: Yellow Mickeys cut from a
Disney brochure; other Mickeys downloaded
from the Internet

"It's So Much Friendlier with Two"
by Heather Armstrong
Claremont, CA
SUPPLIES

Patterned paper: Keeping Memories Alive
Classic Pooh stickers: Michel & Company
Memorabilia idea: Heather included a
wedding proposal and a silhouette
from Disneyland on the layout.

"Disneyland"

by Vicki Garner
Windows of Time
Hooper, UT
SUPPLIES
Patterned paper: The Paper Patch
Computer font: Tech, Print Artist
Mickey Mouse accent and title:
Cut from a Disney shopping bag

"Fantasy in the Sky"

by Valerie Dellastatious
Orem, UT
Photo by Dawn Leighter
Centerville, UT
SUPPLIES
Fireworks paper: Paper Pizazz, Hot Off The Press
Diamond Dust paper: Paper Adventures
Computer fonts: Doodle Cursive (title) and Doodle Tipsy
(journaling), PagePrintables, Cock-A-Doodle Design Inc.

"Disney Fun"

by Jennifer McLaughlin
Back Door Friends—
The Scrapbooking Company
Whittier, CA
Photos by Peggy Peterson
Park City, UT

SUPPLIES
Patterned paper: PrintWorks
Lettering template: Moose
Mountain, D.J. Inkers
Computer font: CK Toggle,
"The Best of Creative Lettering" CD
Vol. 2, *Creating Keepsakes*
Circle punches: Family Treasures

Paper edge: Corkscrew by Fiskars

Disneyland 1999

"Mulan Parade"

Polly Owens

San Antonio, TX

SUPPLIES

Mulberry paper: Handmade Paper, Lacey Company

Computer fonts: Gaze Bold ("Mulan") and
Bangle Bold ("Parade"), True Type Fonts, Bay Animation Inc.

Circle punch: Marvy Uchida

Pen: Zig Writer, EK Success

Dragon paper piecing: Polly's own design

Idea to note: Polly used a craft knife to make the lace art.

"Mulan Parade"

by Lacy Tock

Sonoma, CA

SUPPLIES

Patterned paper: The Paper Patch

Scissors: Alligator edge, Fiskars

"The Mulan Parade"
by Jan Boyd
San Diego, CA
SUPPLIES

Background stamps: Purchased in Chinatown
(the "chops" spell her children's names in Chinese)
Ink pads: Dauber Duos, Tsukineko
Pens: Zig Opaque Writers and Zig Writer,
EK Success; Milky Gel Roller, Pentel
Mulan sticker: Sandylion
Fortune cookie, chopsticks and title letters:
Jan's own designs
Idea to note: Jan took a photo of a parade float
and then put a picture of one of her children
in the middle.

"Mulan Parade"
by Lori Bergmann
Turlock, CA
SUPPLIES

Punches: Marvy Uchida
Hole punch: Punchline, McGill
Pens: Micron Pigma, Sakura; Zig Writer, EK Success
Chalk: Stampin' Up!
Dragon paper piecing: Lori's own design

Paper edge: Corkscrew by Fiskars

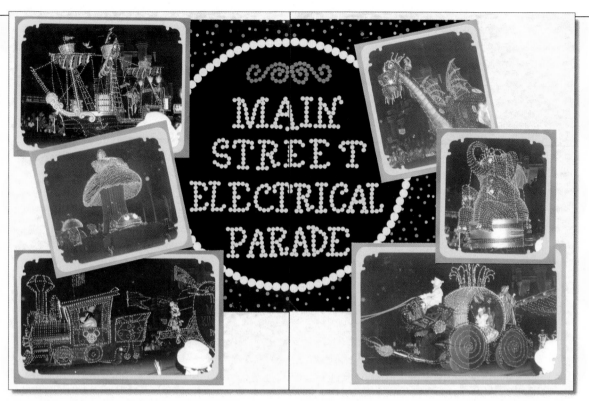

"Main Street Electrical Parade"

by Joeylynn K. Pfeifer
Baltimore, MD
SUPPLIES
Hole punches: Punchline, McGill
Corner punch: Crown, McGill

"Wanted"

by Pam Talluto
Rochester Hills, MI
SUPPLIES
Patterned paper:
The Paper Patch
Scissors: Deckle edge, Fiskars
Star punches: Family Treasures
Stickers: Sandylion
Computer fonts: Wanted and
Country Western Bold, down-
loaded from the Internet; Abadi,
Microsoft Word
*Paper doll, large star and cow-
boy clothes:* Pam's own designs
Memorabilia idea: Pam memori-
alized the fun of the evening by
including the menu and tickets
on the layout.

"Time for Fun"

by Lisa Burk

Puzzle Mates

Brea, CA

SUPPLIES

Clock template: Beach, Puzzle Mates

Number stickers: Making Memories

Mickey Mouse stationery: Paper Pizazz,
Hot Off The Press

Lettering Template: Cut-it-Up

Pens: Zig Writer, EK Success;
Milky Gel Roller, Pentel

"Toy Story"

by Jana Francis

Provo, UT

Photos by Emilee Riley

Salt Lake City, UT

SUPPLIES

Patterned paper: The Paper Patch
(red with white stars);
Frances Meyer (Woody's bandana);
Jana's own design (Woody's shirt);
Paper Adventures (Woody's vest)

Cloud die cuts: Pebbles in my Pocket

Pens: Zig Writers, EK Success

Lettering idea: Jana's own design

*Woody and Mr. Potato Head paper
piecing:* Jana's own designs

Paper edge: Corkscrew by Fiskars

"The Mad Hatters"

by Jennifer Jensen
Hurricane, UT
Photos by Valerie Dellastatious
Orem, UT

SUPPLIES

Patterned paper: The Paper Patch (lavender with white polka dots and turquoise with white polka dots); Colors By Design (purple polka dots on bow)
Lettering template: Block Serif, Pebble Tracers, Pebbles in my Pocket
Daisy punch: Family Treasures
Hole punch: Punchline, McGill
Pen: Zig Writer, EK Success
Mad Hatter paper piecing: Jennifer's own design

Paper-piecing art by Brenée Williams of Boise, ID

PHOTO OP

After your visit to the Mad Hatter store,

put on your silly hats and stack your group

head on head for a totem-pole effect.

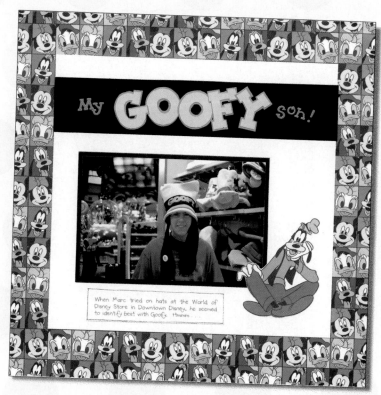

"My Goofy Son"

by Pam Talluto
Rochester Hills, MI

S U P P L I E S

Patterned paper (background): Paper Pizazz, Hot Off The Press

Goofy stationery: Paper Pizazz, Hot Off The Press

Lettering template: Block Serif, Pebble Tracers, Pebbles in my Pocket

Alphabet letters: "Scrapbook" Alphabitties, Repositionable Sticky Die-Cut Letters, Provo Craft

Computer font: CK Toggle, "The Best of Creative Lettering" CD Vol. 2, *Creating Keepsakes*

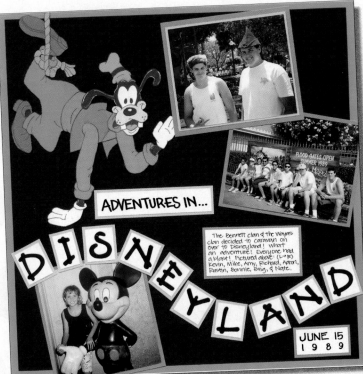

"Adventures in Disneyland"

by Brenda Bennett
Morenci, AZ

S U P P L I E S

Alphabet letters: Kids, Repositionable Sticky Die-Cut Letters, Provo Craft

Pens: Micron Pigma, Sakura; Milky Gel Roller, Pentel

Goofy paper piecing: Brenda got the idea from a Disney storybook.

"Dinner at Chef Mickey's"

by Missy Jaycox

St. Louis, MO

SUPPLIES

Swirl punch: All Night Media

Corner slot punch: Double Scallop, Family Treasures

Pen: Zig Millennium, EK Success

Disney characters: Cut from a souvenir Chef Mickey photo frame (purchased at the restaurant)

Idea to note: Missy made her own patterned paper using a swirl punch, which matches the design on the plate in the photos.

"Happy New Year 2000"

by Alycia Alvarez

Altus, OK

Photos by Laurie Green

Alpine, UT

SUPPLIES

Patterned paper: Frances Meyer (multicolor checkered); Paper Pizazz, Hot Off The Press (purple speckled)

Circle punches (title): Family Treasures

Lettering template (2000): Block Serif, Pebble Tracers, Pebbles in my Pocket

Alphabet letters: "Scrapbook" Alphabitties, Repositionable Sticky Die-Cut Letters, Provo Craft

Rolling pin and bowl die cuts: Pebbles in my Pocket

Photo corners: Canson

Pens: Hybrid Gel Roller and Milky Gel Roller, Pentel

Goofy paper piecing: Adapted from Disney clip art

Paper edge: Corkscrew by Fiskars

"Eating at Goofy's Kitchen"
by Heather Thatcher
Draper, UT
Photos by Laurie Green
Alpine, UT
SUPPLIES
Patterned paper: Provo Craft (striped);
Scrapable Scribbles (polka dot)
Pen: Zig Writer, EK Success
Colored pencils: Prismacolor, Sanford
Computer font: CK Toggle, "The Best of Creative
Lettering" CD Vol. 2, *Creating Keepsakes*
Apron and hat: Heather's own designs

"Breakfast in Bed"
by Brittany Boice
Mom and Me Scrapbooking
Salt Lake City, UT
Photos by Laurie Green
Alpine, UT
SUPPLIES
Alphabet letters: Frances Meyer
Silverware stickers: Mrs. Grossman's
Circle punches: Family Treasures
Pens: Zig Writers, EK Success
Sun, pancakes and orange juice:
Brittany's own designs
Memorabilia idea: Brittany included a
Flex Passport on the layout.

"Mickey Mouse Pancakes"

Shelly Patten
Pebbles in my Pocket
Orem, UT

S U P P L I E S

Patterned paper: Northern Spy
Lettering template: Block, ABC Tracers, EK Success
Circle punches: Family Treasures
Pen: Zig Writer, EK Success
Pancakes: Shelly's own design

"Mickey Cakes"

by Valerie Dellastatious
Orem, UT
Photos by Laurie Green
Alpine, UT

S U P P L I E S

Patterned paper: Keeping Memories Alive
Corrugated paper (bacon): DMD Industries
Lettering template: Block, ABC Tracers, EK Success
Corner slot punch: Family Treasures
Circle die cuts: Pebbles in my Pocket
Computer font: CK Journaling, "The Best of Creative Lettering" CD Vol. 2, *Creating Keepsakes*

"Mickey on a Stick"
by Nancy Church
Augusta, GA
S U P P L I E S
Patterned paper: Close To My Heart/D.O.T.S.
Lettering template: Block, ABC Tracers, EK Success
Circle punch: Family Treasures
Computer font: CK Toggle, "The Best of Creative Lettering" CD Vol. 2, *Creating Keepsakes*
Pen: Zig Writer, EK Success
Mickey popsicles and drips: Nancy's own designs

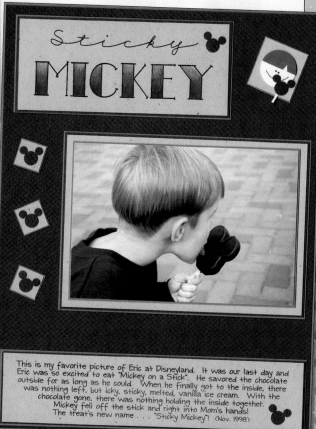

"Sticky Mickey"
by Marla Bird
Pebbles in my Pocket
Orem, UT
S U P P L I E S
Computer font: CK Fill In, "The Best of Creative Lettering" CD Vol. 1; CK Cursive and CK Journaling, "The Best of Creative Lettering" CD Vol. 2, *Creating Keepsakes*
Punches: All Night Media (Mickey); Family Treasures (circle)
Colored pencils: Prismacolor, Sanford
Pen: Zig Writer, EK Success

Vacation Tip

Restaurants at the Disney resorts are busiest between 11:00 a.m. and 2:00 p.m. and from 5:00 p.m. to 7:00 p.m. If you snack throughout the day, and visit the restaurants during the off hours, you'll be able to get a table more readily.

Paper edge: Corkscrew by Fiskars

DiSNeYLaNd '99

Susan, Alyssa and Emsley — 3 generations of mouse ears!

SIMBA SIMBA SIMBA SIMBA

Susan, Alyssa, Emsley, Meleah, Kamryn, David and I all went to Disneyland for a day while we were visiting San Juan Capistrano. Lunch was a hillbilly/ comedy act ☺

READMISSION CARD
VALID ONLY ON:
08/09/99
THIS CARD AND A VALID HANDSTAMP ARE REQUIRED FOR RE-ENTRY TO DISNEYLAND.

NON-TRANSFERABLE
NOT FOR SALE

"Disneyland '99"

by Becky Higgins
Peoria, AZ
SUPPLIES
Vellum and Diamond Dust paper:
Paper Adventures
Colored pencils: Prismacolor, Sanford
Pen: Zig Writer, EK Success

Circle punches: McGill
Idea to note: Becky used
photos from brochures and catalogs
as layout accents.
Memorabilia idea: Becky included the
park readmission cards on the layout.

Paper edge: Corkscrew by Fiskars

"Disney Friends"
by Heather Thatcher
Draper, UT
SUPPLIES
Diamond Dust paper: Paper Adventures
Mickey hand die cut: Dayco
Border template: Rectangles, Provo Craft
Colored pencils: Prismacolor, Sanford
Pen: Zig Writer, EK Success
Lettering idea: Heather's own design

"Fairy Tales Do Come True"
by Brenda Bennett
Morenci, AZ
Photos by Emilee Riley
Salt Lake City, UT
SUPPLIES
Patterned paper: PrintWorks
Lettering template: Classic, Pebble
Tracers, Pebbles in my Pocket
Computer font: CK Journaling, "The Best of Creative
Lettering" CD Vol. 2, *Creating Keepsakes*
Colored pencils: Prismacolor, Sanford
Ink pad (sponged around journaling boxes): Stampin' Up!
Castle: Brenda modified a die cut from Accu-Cut
Systems to create her paper-pieced castle.

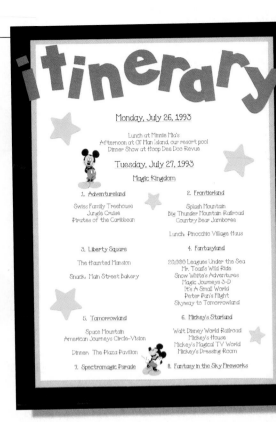

itinerary

Monday, July 26, 1993

Lunch at Minnie Miu's
Afternoon at Ol' Man Island, our resort pool
Dinner Show at Hoop Dee Doo Revue

Tuesday, July 27, 1993

Magic Kingdom

1. Adventureland

Swiss Family Treehouse
Jungle Cruise
Pirates of the Caribbean

2. Frontierland

Splash Mountain
Big Thunder Mountain Railroad
Country Bear Jamboree

Lunch: Pinocchio Village Haus

3. Liberty Square

The Haunted Mansion

Snack: Main Street Bakery

4. Fantasyland

20,000 Leagues Under the Sea
Mr. Toad's Wild Ride
Snow White's Adventures
Magic Journeys 3-D
It's A Small World
Peter Pan's Flight
Skyway to Tomorrowland

5. Tomorrowland

Space Mountain
American Journeys Circle-Vision

Dinner: The Plaza Pavilion

6. Mickey's Starland

Walt Disney World Railroad
Mickey's House
Mickey's Magical TV World
Mickey's Dressing Room

7. Spectromagic Parade

8. Fantasy in the Sky Fireworks

Wednesday, July 28, 1993

Disney-MGM Studios

Indiana Jones Stunt Spectacular
Star Tours
Beauty and the Beast
Muppet Vision 3D
Teenage Mutant Ninja Turtles
The Great Movie Ride
Voyage of the Little Mermaid
Backstage Studio Tour with Catastrophe Canyon

Aladdin's Royal Caravan Parade

Sorcery in the Sky Fireworks

Lunch: Soundstage Restaurant featuring Aladdin
Snack: Backlot Express
Dinner: Acadian Pizza 'n Pasta at Dixie Landings

Thursday, July 29, 1993

Boat Ride to Disney Village Marketplace

Disney Village Marketplace

Shopping at Mickey's Character Shop
Snack at Lakeside Terrace

"Itinerary"

by Pam Talluto
Rochester Hills, MI

SUPPLIES

Lettering template: Block, ABC Tracers, EK Success
Punches: All Night Media (Mickey Mouse); Family Treasures (stars)
Stickers: Sandylion
Computer font: DJ Squared, Fontastic! Vol. 1, D.J. Inkers

"The Long Ride"

by Pam Talluto
Rochester Hills, MI

SUPPLIES

Patterned paper: The Paper Patch (checked); Paper Pizazz, Hot Off The Press (road signs)
Vellum and metallic paper: Paper Adventures
Star and circle punches: Family Treasures
Car die cut: Ellison
Mickey stickers: Sandylion
Computer fonts: CK Anything Goes, "The Best of Creative Lettering" CD Vol. 1, *Creating Keepsakes* (title); DJ Squared, Fontastic! Vol. 1 and DJ Squirrelly, Fontastic! Vol. 2, D.J. Inkers
Pens: Tombow

"Off to Disneyland"

by Amber Blakesley
Provo, UT
Photos by Laurie Green
Alpine, UT
SUPPLIES
Patterned paper: The Paper Patch
Alphabet Letter and bird stickers:
Mary Engelbreit, InterArt
Dist./Sunrise

Flower die cuts: Ellison
Circle punch: Marvy Uchida
Hole punch: Punchline, McGill
Pens: Zig Writers, EK Success
Design tip: Amber unified the
layout by decorating the photo
frames and the journaling block
to match the Mary Engelbreit
letter stickers.

PHOTO OP

Don't forget the vacation adventures you enjoyed outside

the Disney park. Get photos of your group waiting in the airport, during the

flight and returning home. You may even want to take pictures in front of

your hotel and in your room. Finally, be sure to include airline tickets,

receipts and rental-car information in your scrapbook.

"All Ears"

by Bonnie Blumenstock
Pebbles in my Pocket
Orem, UT

SUPPLIES

Patterned paper (polka dots): The Paper Patch
Lettering template: Block, ABC Tracers, EK Success
Pen: Gelly Roll, Sakura
Mickey die cut: Bonnie created her own design using the circle ruler by EK Success.
Idea to note: Bonnie created her own "Mickey Mouse" patterned paper using the Minnie font from Microsoft Word on her computer.

Heather and Brenda...

ALL EARS

"I Want to Go to Disneyland Again"

by Carlyn Wootton
Springville, UT

SUPPLIES

Patterned paper: The Paper Patch
(polka dots, hearts, yellow plaid);
Northern Spy (red and blue plaids)
Lettering template: Block Serif,
Pebble Tracers, Pebbles in my Pocket
Computer font: DJ Squared, Fontastic!
Vol. 1, D.J. Inkers
Mickey paper piecing: Idea from a sports water bottle purchased at Disneyland.

"Disneyland"

by Stephanie Barnard
Puzzle Mates
Brea, CA

SUPPLIES

Alphabet die cuts: Scrapbook, Accu-Cut Systems
Mickey ears template: Rain, Puzzle Mates
Pen: Zig Writer, EK Success
Girl: Stephanie's own design

"Disney Christmas"

by Pam Talluto

Rochester Hills, MI

SUPPLIES

Patterned paper: Provo Craft (snowflakes); The Paper Patch (small red and white polka dots)

Lettering template: Block, ABC Tracers, EK Success

Photo frame: Frame-Ups, My Mind's Eye

Kids: Friends, My Mind's Eye

Snowflake punch: Family Treasures

"Christmas Is for the Dogs"

by Lori Bergmann

Turlock, CA

Photos by Laurie Green

Alpine, UT

SUPPLIES

Punches: McGill (oak leaf, holly); Family Treasures (circles)

Dalmatian stickers: Sandylion

Alphabet letters: "Fat Dot," Repositionable Sticky Die-Cut Letters, Provo Craft

Dalmatian and bones paper piecing: Idea from Dalmatian stickers

Pens: Zig Writers, EK Success

Idea to note: Lori used a shoelace on the layout to echo the garland decorations in the photos.

"Shopping at Disney Village Marketplace"

by Pam Talluto
Rochester Hills, MI
SUPPLIES
Patterned paper:
The Paper Patch
Lettering template: Block,
ABC Tracers, EK Success
Tree template: Provo Craft
Scissors: Deckle and
Scallop edges, Fiskars
Stickers: Sandylion

Computer font: DJ Squared,
Fontastic! Vol. 1, D.J. Inkers
Boat and shopping bags:
Pam's own designs
Other: Pam used tissue
paper and embroidery floss
on the shopping bags.
Memorabilia idea: Pam
included a Disney Dollar
and pictures from a Disney
brochure on the layout.

"Our Story"
by Debbie Vaccaro
Campbell, CA
SUPPLIES
Wavy ruler: Creative Memories
Stickers: Mrs. Grossman's (school, car,
food, castle, pirates, carousel, tea cups,
tree and ticket booth); Heartline, Hallmark Cards
(Winnie the Pooh, Tigger and Piglet);
Sandylion (Sleeping Beauty and fairies,
small Winnie the Pooh, Aurora and rabbit)
Pen: Creative Memories

We're going to
DISNEYLAND

"We're Going to Disneyland"
by Karan Simoni
Antioch, CA
SUPPLIES

Patterned paper: The Paper Patch (polka dots and checked); Frances Meyer (tree trunks); Provo Craft (asphalt)
Punches: Family Treasures
Pens: Zig Millennium and Zig Opaque Writers, EK Success; Hybrid Gel Rollers, Pentel
Computer fonts: CK Fill In, "The Best of Creative Lettering" CD Vol. 1, *Creating Keepsakes*; Scrap Simple, Lettering Delights Vol. 2, Inspire Graphics
Car: Karan's used a coloring book for the pattern.
Idea to note: Karan made the sunglasses by cutting a heart punch in half.

"Disneyland"
by Kerri Bradford
Orem, UT
SUPPLIES

Patterned paper: Provo Craft (blue striped); Robin's Nest (yellow); Scrap Pads, Provo Craft (green bushes)
Lettering template: Zoom, Close To My Heart/D.O.T.S.
Flower punch: Mini Punch, All Night Media
Hole and teardrop punches: Punchline, McGill
Scissors: Deckle edge, Fiskars
Pens: Zig Writers, EK Success
Idea to note: Kerri got her idea for the layout from a souvenir book.

PHOTO OP
You've probably noticed the Mickey Mouse head in the flowering garden at Disneyland's entrance. This is a perfect spot for group photos.

Our templates are real lifesavers.

Introducing Jill's Paper Doll World™ Templates.

Now you can create paper dolls wherever and whenever you want. With this new collection of templates, you can choose from the basic template with the doll and hair, or four seasonal templates full of clothing and accessories. Simply trace and cut to create the look you want. And since the template designs are the same size and shape as Jill's Paper Doll World dies, you can interchange clothes and accessories with ease. Go ahead—go overboard!

Ask for Jill's Paper Doll World Templates at your favorite craft retail store, visit **www.accucut.com** or call **800-288-1670**.

Jill's Paper Doll World™ **from**

Making it easy. Making it fun.™

Picture Your Memories On Printed Background Papers By:

The Paper Patch®

Over 500 Printed Backgrounds To Choose From!

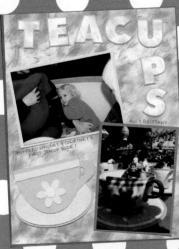

Mix & Match our 8½" x 11", and 12" x 12" original and basic prints.

For wholesale information please
call: 801-253-3018

Page layouts by Wendy Bird at: wendybird@gonescrappin.com

by Alyssa Allgaier

Capture Your Magical Moments on Film

Make your

photos "click"

with these

easy tips

ONE SUREFIRE WAY TO GET GREAT photos is to look for the "Kodak Picture Spot" signs throughout the Disney resorts. But before you go, check out these tips to ensure that you get some outstanding photos.

◆ Give each of your children a disposable camera, and encourage them to capture their favorite scenes. See the magic through their eyes!

◆ Strategically place your "designated photographer" before the action begins. You may want to have the photographer sit two seats ahead of you on a ride, for example. This helps to avoid big white faces and dark backgrounds.

◆ Ask the person next to you in line to take a photo of you and your group. This way, the family photographer (aka you) can be in some photos too!

◆ Stop by Guest Relations and find out where the park cameras are located. The photos cost $10, but it may be worth it to have a nice group shot where everyone is looking straight at the camera!

◆ Be ready to snap your photos quickly. Rather than holding up the whole ride, plan your photos ahead of time—then aim, focus and shoot.

◆ The resorts offer a variety of interactive activities. Be sure to get photos of your group participating in these activities.

◆ Once the ride is over, hop off quickly and get a shot of your family before they disembark.

◆ Pick up postcards that have good shots of your favorite attractions. Think of them as insurance, in case some of your photos aren't up to par.

◆ Every time you visit the park, take photos of family members standing next to their favorite rides. As the years pass, make "then and now" layouts (see Figure 1).

There you have it, nine easy photo tips that'll help you capture all the spontaneity of your trip. ♥

Figure 1. Add historical perspective to your scrapbook by incorporating "then" and "now" photos in one layout. *Pages by Becky Higgins.* **Supplies** *Patterned paper:* Provo Craft (plaid); Carolee's Creations (antique); *Lettering template:* Block Serif, Pebble Tracers, Pebbles in my Pocket; *Circle punch:* McGill; *Computer font:* CK Toggle, "The Best of Creative Lettering" CD Vol. 2, *Creating Keepsakes.*

Paper edge: Corkscrew by Fiskars

from
shoe boxes
to family
treasures…

Layout by: Jennifer McLaughlin; Photos by: Peggy Peterson and Don Lambson. Disney Characters © Disney Enterprises, Inc.

A magical TEA party

Levi and Tana love riding Dumbo the Flying Elephant and the Mad Tea Party. Tana loves the colorful cups and we love to watch her spin and giggle.

We'll show you how!

Discover the pleasure of creating a family treasure!

Whether you're a beginning scrapbooker or a seasoned pro, *Creating Keepsakes* scrapbook magazine has everything you need to organize and creatively present your treasured memories. You don't need a lot of time, talent or money to get started! It's fun using archival papers and today's new specialized scrapbooking products. Enjoy the new product reviews and experiment with

techniques from the experts. You'll love our Creative Lettering column with easy-to-follow instructions. Plus, each issue is jam-packed with oodles of fantastic scrapbook page examples. Start organizing and preserving your family's memories to last through the generations with a little help from the recognized scrapbooking authority—*Creating Keepsakes* scrapbook magazine!

Send for Your FREE Issue Today!
Don't let your precious memories fade away.

Take advantage of this Special No-Risk Offer!
New subscribers—send for your free trial issue today! If you like what you see, you'll get an additional nine issues for the low subscription rate of $22.97. That's a savings of 54% off the cover price!

Please fill out the attached card and send it in right away or for faster service visit us on the web at www.creatingkeepsakes.com, or you can call us at 888/247-5282

CREATING
Keepsakes
SCRAPBOOK MAGAZINE

The Scrapbooking Authority!

B00AA-5

DISNEY
AT HOME

Sarah loves to dress up.
She was excited to have
her very own puppy coat
and wig like Cruella De Vil.
She tried so hard to look
mean like Cruella but she
just couldn't do it. She's
too cute to be mean!

"Cruella De Vil"
by Candy Clay
Blue Springs, MO

S U P P L I E S

Patterned paper: Making Memories
Paper doll: Jill's Paper Doll World, Accu-Cut Systems
101 Dalmatians accent: Downloaded from the Internet
Computer font: CK Journaling, "The Best of Creative Lettering"
CD Vol. 2, *Creating Keepsakes*
Pen: Zig Writer, EK Success
Other: Candy decorated the paper doll with
"fur" to look like Cruella De Vil.

Paper-piecing art by Brenée Williams of Boise, ID

"Your Dalmatian Costume"

by Brittany Boice
Mom and Me Scrapbooking
Salt Lake City, UT
Photos by Cindy Yip
San Diego, CA

S U P P L I E S

Patterned paper: Keeping Memories Alive (grass);
Brittany's own design (red-and-black border)
Grass die cuts: Pebbles in my Pocket
Paper doll: Accu-Cut Systems
Punches: Family Treasures (circles, heart balloon,
paw, bone and flower); source unknown (tulip)
Hole punch: Punchline, McGill
Pen: Zig Writer, EK Success
Doghouse and dog mask: Brittany's own designs

"Dalmatian Celebration"

by Christine Baker
Palmdale, CA
S U P P L I E S

Patterned paper: The Paper Patch
Pens: Zig Writers, EK Success
Colored pencils: Memory Pencils, EK Success
Dalmatian and lettering ideas: Christine's own designs

"Our Snow White"

by Kristin Mill
Indianapolis, IN

SUPPLIES

Gold frame: remember when . . ., Colorbök
Birds and flowers: Disney clip art
Computer font (journaling): Kaufmann, Print Shop
Title and caption lettering: Kristin's own ideas
Pens: Zig Writer, EK Success (black);
Fibracolor (colored)
Snow White paper piecing: Kristin got the
idea from a Disney coloring book.

"Once Upon a Time"

by Melle Broaderick
Ocala, FL

SUPPLIES

Patterned paper: Creative Memories
Star die cuts: Creative Memories
Star and ribbon stickers: Mrs. Grossman's
Computer font: Monotype Cursiva, Print Shop

Paper edge: Corkscrew by Fiskars

"'Belle' of the Ball"

by Erin Terrell
San Antonio, TX
Photos by Laurie Green
Alpine, UT

SUPPLIES

Patterned paper: Paper Adventures
Lettering template: Tam's Wacky, Cut-it-Up
Pen: Zig Opaque Writer, EK Success
Colored pencils: Memory Pencils, EK Success
Idea to note: Erin printed the image of Belle
(which she downloaded from the Internet)
and colored it with pencils.

"Brooke's Cinderella Party"

by Cheryl Jorgensen
Albuquerque, NM

SUPPLIES

Paper doll: Jill's Paper Doll World, Accu-Cut Systems
Vellum: The Paper Company
Computer font: CK Anything Goes, "The Best of Creative
Lettering" CD Vol. 1 and CK Cursive, "The Best of Creative
Lettering" CD Vol. 2, *Creating Keepsakes*
Spiral punch: McGill
Paper doll's dress: Cheryl's own design
Glass slipper invitation: Cheryl's own design

Hug a little....   Love a little....

Laugh a lot.....   Oh!

I Just Can't WAIT to Be KING!

Halloween 1999

"Hug a Little, Love a Little"
by Tammy Cooper
Mesa, AZ

S U P P L I E S

Patterned paper: Keeping Memories Alive
Classic Pooh stickers: Michel & Company
Punches: All Night Media (Winnie the Pooh);
Family Treasures (flowers and butterflies)
Computer font: DJ Bassoon,
Fontastic! Vol. 1, D.J. Inkers
Pen: Zig Millennium, EK Success

"I Just Can't Wait to Be King"
by Michelle Gowan
Macon, GA

S U P P L I E S

Specialty paper: Paper Adventures (velvet);
Personal Stamp Exchange (mulberry paper)
Alphabet letters: "Kids," Repositionable
Sticky Die-Cut Letters, Provo Craft
Punches: Family Treasures

Paper edge: Corkscrew by Fiskars

101 Dalmations is one of Elizabeth's favorite Disney movies. Her favorite thing to do is play with all the little toy dalmations that we've collected over the years. She also likes to read the books. At night, she usually sleeps with one of the stuffed puppies.

101 TONS OF FUN

"101 Tons of Fun"
by Beth Wakulsky
Haslett, MI
SUPPLIES

Lettering templates: Block Serif, Pebble Tracers, Pebbles in my Pocket
Pens: Micron Pigma, Sakura; Tombow
Dalmatians: Beth traced the Dalmatians from a Little Golden Book coloring book.
Patterned paper: Beth made the patterned paper using a black pen.

"The Disney Store"

by Kimberly Y. Smith
Reddick, FL
SUPPLIES

Computer fonts: CK Script, "The Best of Creative Lettering" CD Vol. 1; CK Simplicity and CK Journaling, "The Best of Creative Lettering" CD Vol. 2, *Creating Keepsakes*

Mickey Mouse stickers: Sandylion
Paper doll (head): Stick People, Stamping Station
Mickey Mouse accent: Color copy of a Disney ad
Heart punch: McGill
Pens: Gelly Rolls, Sakura

Memorable Magic Moments
The Disney Store

Adrien went on a field trip to see Santa Claus at the Oaks Mall in Gainesville, FL. While touring the Mall, he visited The Disney Store. Adrien is a big fan of Disney. Here are some pictures of his memorable, magic moments at The Disney Store.

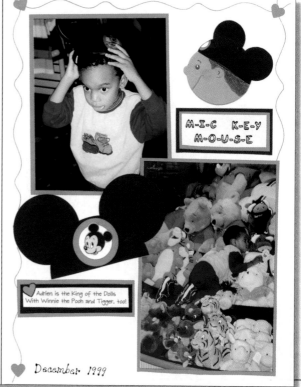

M-I-C K-E-Y M-O-U-S-E

Adrien is the King of the Dolls With Winnie the Pooh and Tigger, too!

December 1999

"Party"

by Rhonda Scott
Fairfield, CA

S U P P L I E S

Lettering template:
Wacky Letters, Frances Meyer
Vellum: The Paper Company
Winnie the Pooh paper piecing:
Rhonda got the idea from a
Disney coloring book.
Idea to note: Rhonda used
Pop Dots from All Night Media
to add dimension to the accents.

"Pooh and My Hunny"

by Pamela James
Evanston, IL

S U P P L I E S

Patterned paper: The Paper Patch
Metallic paper: Paper Cuts
Winnie the Pooh accents:
Punch-Outs, Hot Off The Press
Stickers: Provo Craft
Star punch: Punchline, McGill
Velveteen and vellum paper:
Paper Adventures
Computer font: GrantsHand, Print Artist
Honey pot: Pamela's own design

"Winnie the Pooh"

by Jana Francis
Provo, UT

S U P P L I E S

Patterned paper: The Paper Patch
Alphabet letters: "Kids," Repositionable
Sticky Die-Cut Letters, Provo Craft
Pen: Zig Writer, EK Success
Winnie the Pooh and tree paper piecing:
Jana's own designs

"Peek-a-Boo"
by Karen Towery
Dallas, GA
SUPPLIES
Winnie the Pooh stationery:
Paper Pizazz, Hot Off The Press
Swirl punch: All Night Media
Computer fonts: DJ Squared, Fontastic!
Vol. 1, D.J. Inkers (journaling);
Comic Sans, Microsoft Office (title)

The Little Boy
in the Mirror

Jack found a new
friend in our hotel
room in Chattanooga.
He said "hi" to him,
played peekaboo, and
even gave him a kiss.

"Baby Goofy Meets Baby Kurtis"
by Nancy Mar
Vancouver, BC, Canada
SUPPLIES
Patterned paper: Keeping Memories Alive
Circle punch: Family Treasures
Chalk: Craf-T Products
Pen: Zig Writer, EK Success
Title, Goofy, car, toys and blocks: Nancy's own designs

"Frankie Meets His Favorite Cowboy"
by Bee Rozatti
Corona, CA
SUPPLIES
Toy Story accents: Bee took photos of pictures
in her son's *Toy Story* book. She cropped
the images and included them on the layout.
Pen: Milky Gel Roller, Pentel
Hole punch: Punchline, McGill

Frankie meets his
favorite cowboy, Woody!
"Toy Story" the movie is a
hit with our boys. Three
months later for Halloween...
these photos say it all!

CALLAHAN
AND
BUZZ LIGHTYEAR
OCTOBER 1999

"To Infinity and Beyond"

by Jami Eldredge-Blackham
Salt Lake City, UT

SUPPLIES

Lettering template: Block, ABC Tracers, EK Success

Pens: Milky Gel Roller, Pentel;
Zig Millennium, EK Success

Colored pencils: Crayola

Buzz Lightyear paper piecing:
Jami got the idea from a Disney coloring book.

"Grandpa Kuhn Has His Own Toy Story"

by Pam Kuhn
Bryan, OH

SUPPLIES

Patterned paper: Keeping Memories Alive (speckled); The Paper Patch (Woody's bandana); Pam's own design (Woody's shirt)

Lettering templates: Rounded, Pebble Tracers, Pebbles in my Pocket ("Toy"); Scrapbook, Provo Craft ("Story")

Computer font: CK Print, "The Best of Creative Lettering" CD Vol. 1, *Creating Keepsakes*

Hole and star punches: Punchline, McGill

Pens: Milky Gel Roller, Pentel; Zig Memory System, EK Success

Woody paper piecing: Pam's own design

Movie clapboard: Pam's own design

Paper edge: Corkscrew by Fiskars

12·18·99

Grandpa Kuhn has his own toy story!

Family Toys – Family Bonds

Grandpa Kuhn has collected Disney toys for quite awhile. The brown mouse (upper left) belonged to Grandpa's grandfather. Grandpa remembers playing with it when he was about 5 years old. He was always told that this was one of the first designs for Mickey Mouse. If you examine it closely, the red shorts and smile are still trademark characteristics in today's Mickey.

Grandpa Kuhn shows dad how one of his favorite toys works (lower left) In the front of this collection, Addy and Becca brought out some of their Disney "collectibles" to show off.

Dad, Grandpa, Addy, and Becca have a tea party with Grandpa's antique Mickey tea set (upper right). This is the first tea party you have had with Grandpa.

It was really neat to talk about all of our family memories of Disney toys. We heard stories from four generations! We hope that the special toys stay in the family.

TOY STORY

"Beauty and the Beast"

by Beth Wakulsky
Haslett, MI
Photos by Emilee Riley
Salt Lake City, UT
SUPPLIES
Punches: Punchline, McGill
(circle); Family Treasures (spiral)

Oval template: Creative Memories
Pen: Zig Opaque Writer,
EK Success
Computer fonts: EnglischeScht
and BaskervilleOldFacSCD,
Print Artist
Flowers: Beth's own designs

"Tyler's First Birthday"

by Heidi Prince
Cumming, GA
SUPPLIES
Alphabet letters: "Kids,"
Repositionable Sticky Die-Cut
Letters, Provo Craft
Bee rub-ons: Provo Craft
Scissors: Deckle edge, Fiskars
Teardrop punch: Punchline, McGill

Computer font: Scrap Serif,
Lettering Delights Vol. 1,
Inspire Graphics
"Hunny" pots and sign: Heidi
scanned Winnie the Pooh wrapping paper from Tyler's birthday
party and enlarged the images.

"First Trip to the Movies"
by Terrie McDaniel
League City, TX

SUPPLIES

Patterned paper: Frances Meyer (leopard);
The Paper Patch (red and white striped)
Scissors: Deckle edge, Fiskars
Popcorn bucket and ticket die cuts: Ellison
Flower punch (popcorn): All Night Media
Computer fonts: CK Fill In, "The Best of Creative
Lettering" CD Vol. 1, *Creating Keepsakes* (title);
Lucida Handwriting, Microsoft Word (journaling)
Pens: Zig Writer and Zig Scroll & Brush, EK Success
Tarzan accents: Scanned from the
Tarzan soundtrack cover.

"I Wanna Be with You"
by Linda Strauss
Provo, UT

SUPPLIES

Alphabet letters: "Scrapbook" Alphabitties,
Repositionable Sticky Die-Cut Letters, Provo Craft
Paper piecing: Linda's own designs

Paper edge: Corkscrew by Fiskars

The Finishing Touch

Keeping

the focus

on your

photos

Y OU'VE SPENT HOURS SELECTING THE perfect colors to complement your photos, turning your favorite into a strong focal point and arranging them with your journaling so they flow smoothly. Now comes the finishing touch: your enhancements. But how do you ensure that they really do "enhance"—rather than dominate—your page? Read on to learn some tried-and-true enhancement tips.

LIMIT ENHANCEMENTS

If you've spent any time at all in a scrapbook store, you know that a dizzying array of enhancements is available. But how do you use these wonderful products without overwhelming your photos?

◆ **Limit the number of enhancements on each layout.** Don't feel obligated to use an entire sheet of stickers on one layout. Decide which enhancements best suit your current needs, and file the others for future use.

◆ **Limit the number of enhancement themes on each layout.** Although your photos may encompass a variety of events or activities, your layout will be more cohesive and appealing if you select one enhancement theme.

PAY ATTENTION TO PROPORTION

Scrutinize your photographs before you select enhancements. The size of your enhancements should be determined relative to the size of a photo's subject. Here are two ways to ensure that your enhancements are in proportion:

◆ **Build a scene.** If you've found the perfect sticker or craft punch to enhance your layout but find it's too small by itself, simply build a scene by grouping several items together.

◆ **Change the size.** Thanks to all of the high-tech products on the market, you're never limited to the original size of stickers, die cuts, rubber stamps and other enhancements. By using a color copier, you can easily enlarge or shrink enhancement images to make them proportional to other elements of your layout.

Once you've selected the right enhancements for your layout, it's time to incorporate them. Place them in a triangle that encompasses the entire layout, thus guiding the viewer's eye naturally to each component of your design.

Remember, adding the right enhancement can gracefully unify your layout's theme and rhythm. But watch out: The wrong enhancement can draw attention away from your most cherished items—the photos. When in doubt, err on the side of simplicity. ♥

Placing enhancements in a visual triangle helps to lead the eye through the layout. *Page by Kristy Banks of Highland, UT.* **Supplies** *Punches:* Family Treasures; *Photo frame:* O' Scrap!, Imaginations!; *Patterned paper:* The Paper Patch; *Computer fonts:* Doodle Summer (title), PagePrintables, Cock-A-Doodle Design Inc.; CK Journaling, "The Best of Creative Lettering" CD Vol. 2, *Creating Keepsakes.*

Paper edge: Corkscrew by Fiskars

by Tracy White

Visiting with Friends

*I*n September 1998,

Lanae Johnson and her husband

took their 4-year-old daughter,

Jaena, to Disneyland. "Jaena was

so happy. She danced through the

park like she had springs on her

feet," recalls Lanae. "Every time she

saw a character, her face would

light up." Lanae loves this photo

because Jaena and Dale look so

comfortable with each other—

"It's like they're buddies."

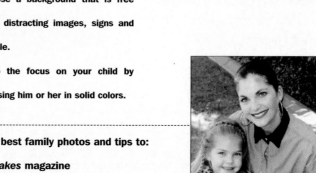

To capture such priceless moments like a pro:

- **Avoid harsh shadows by using the fill flash on your camera.**
- **Ask the character to sit or kneel so that you can really zero in on his and your child's faces.**

- **Choose a background that is free from distracting images, signs and people.**
- **Keep the focus on your child by dressing him or her in solid colors.**

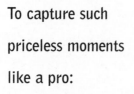

Lanae and her daughter, Jaena

Do you "get the picture"? Send copies of your best family photos and tips to:

Parting Shot • *Creating Keepsakes* magazine

354 Mountain Way Drive • Orem, UT 84058

Paper edge: Corkscrew by Fiskars